Getting Ready for AACR 2

THE CATALOGER'S GUIDE

by Christa F.B. Hoffmann

Serials examples by Sally C. Tseng

Knowledge Industry Publications, Inc.
White Plains, New York

Professional Librarian Series

Getting Ready for AACR 2: The Cataloger's Guide

Library of Congress Cataloging in Publication Data

Hoffmann, Christa F B
  Getting ready for AACR 2.

  (Professional librarian series)
  Includes index.
  1. Descriptive cataloging. 2. Anglo-American
cataloguing rules, 2d ed. I. Title. II. Series.
Z694.H627   025.3 '2   80-15168
ISBN 0-914236-64-4 (pbk.)

Material from *Anglo-American Cataloguing Rules,* second edition, is quoted by permission of the American Library Association; copyright © 1978 by the American Library Association, Canadian Library Association and the Library Association.

Printed in the United States of America

Table of Contents

List of Tables and Figures

List of Cataloging Examples and Illustrations

Monographs (illustrations on pages 60-83)

I

Introduction

Before launching into what this guide to the second edition of the *Anglo-American Cataloguing Rules* (AACR 2)[1] is about, let us briefly state what it is not. Foremost, it is not another critique. The code has been criticized sufficiently, before and after its publication; one can safely assume that other critiques will follow when the code is being applied in earnest. We should also remember that the code is the work of a group of people, a committee, and has it not been said that "a camel is a horse designed by a committee"? But we should recognize that camels can be very useful animals under the right circumstances.

In all seriousness, the code has more merits than shortcomings and is much more user-oriented than AACR 1. It is the user for whom, let us hope, we are producing the catalog.

AACR 2 is also much more logically arranged, and consequently easier to use, than any of the previous codes. The mnemonic numbering in the second and third levels of the rules allows us to move with some speed from format to format.

It is easy to dismiss some critiques, which consider only a particular part of the rules and not a following provision which may also be applied. The concern has been expressed, for example, that Hans Christian Andersen must now be entered as H.C. Andersen because that is the way his name may appear on the title page. But there are just as many items with the full name, Hans Christian Andersen, on the title page, and the basic provision under choice of name permits entry under the most frequently and/or best-known form. We may securely keep that spinner of a fabulous yarn under the form of the name so familiar to most of us.

In fact, at the 1980 Annual American Library Association Conference (New York) it was learned that LC is indeed establishing this entry as "Andersen, H.C. (Hans Christian), 1805-1875," since that apparently is the predominantly cited form in Danish reference sources. The interpretation is that if the title pages do not provide conclusive evidence of the predominant form, the name will be established as it is most frequently cited in reference sources of the writer's country of origin. This extends to authors the provision of Rule 22.1B (second sentence) which applies specifically to a person working "in a nonverbal context (e.g., a painter, a sculptor) or . . . not known primarily as an author . . ." The rationale for this interpretation is that LC is also cataloging for an international community; that this method of selection assures consistency in establishing names and is not dependent on a cataloging librarian's national origin; and that using the reference sources of a writer's, artist's, producer's, etc. country of origin helps to ensure that only one form of heading is established. It is hoped that this method will further universal bibliographic control and efficient interchange of bibliographic data.

Some of the perceived shortcomings of AACR 2 are already being addressed by the large national libraries in the United States, Canada, the United Kingdom and Australia. There seems to be agreement, for example, to continue entering maps under the corporate body and not to follow AACR 2, which would require entry under title for most maps since none of the rules permitting entry under the corporate body would generally apply.[2] Another practical issue is the need to differentiate between identical titles of serials and series. The Library of Congress (LC) and the National Library of Canada are proposing a rule addition which would create a unique title for these materials.

Thus the rules are already changing, even before we in the field have begun to apply them. It will become very important to keep abreast of the evolutionary transformation of the rules. The last chapter of this guide cites sources which librarians should consult for the most current information.

For some librarians, the new code is a radical departure from the past, particularly in its provisions for new ISBD punctuation and spacing. For others, the changes do not adequately consider the machine manipulation of bibliographic records. This guide considers the first issue in Chapter V, which deals with the pattern of prescribed punctuation and the rationale for that punctuation. It will not, however, discuss the latter issue. The MARC (MAchine Readable Cataloging) formats themselves have been criticized for following too closely the conventional 3 x 5 catalog card concepts and for taking insufficient advantage of the capabilities that machine manipulation of bibliographic data affords the library world. Moreover, the MARC formats have been and are being revised, in order to accommodate AACR 2. Some of these revisions are not yet completed, and not all the data has been published.

What, then, is the purpose of this book? It is an effort to help you get ready to apply AACR 2 in your library. It offers a practical approach to this task. AACR 2 should force us to look at our procedures and policies and to make the necessary changes so that we are ready by Day 1 (January 2, 1981). To help you accomplish these objectives, this book provides tables for recording your decisions and for subsequent use as a ready reference in your work.

Some of us may only be responsible for processing one or two formats; however, many of us must deal with nearly the full gamut of them. In either case, the decisions should be consistently applied. It is almost more important to be consistent than to be right, so that others who use our products can do so more efficiently. The tables presented here may also serve as a suggestion for you to develop your own tables, again to achieve consistency of application within a department and for yourself.

The book, as can be discerned from the table of contents, follows AACR 2 make-up. It deals first with the descriptive aspects of the code and then with the access points. A glossary of terminology (Chapter II) precedes actual discussion of the code.

Description under AACR 2 has a new form, given to it by the prescribed punctuation. It has made a radical departure from previous rules, although AACR 1 Chapter 6, revised (published in 1974)[3] contained 90% of the changes. The remaining 10% comprise changes in the note punctuation and an addition to the edition area. Also, of course, the AACR 2 rule numbers differ. Punctuation, like most parts of the rules, follows a general pattern. Once this pattern is recognized and mastered, it can be applied efficiently and will help in any subfield coding for those who are inputting records in bibliographic data bases (e.g., OCLC).

Chapter VI illustrates the changes and similarities brought about by AACR 2 by presenting a large number of actual cataloging examples. Two bibliographic records are provided to enable you to compare the differences. The first record is in AACR 2 form; the second reflects the cataloging rules in effect at the time the item was issued. Often these examples are LC cataloging copy. In the discussion that follows each example, we present the changes and the rules we applied to arrive at the record under consideration. As an additional aid, each example is accompanied by a copy of its chief source of information, e.g., a title page or disc label. From this data you should be able to make further comparisons between the old and the new formats of the records for the same bibliographic item. These primary sources of information should be particularly useful when you try to follow the changes in a particular record, especially in cases where we have tried to illustrate the flexibility of the new code by applying a provision from the general rules (see Example M12, *A Manual of the Writings in Middle English, 1050-1500*).

The examples emphasize monographs, although microforms, serials, music and sound recordings have not been neglected. The cause, no doubt, is the author's own experience and environment, which is still book-oriented. However, this choice permitted us to select a variety of problems for which solutions had to be found under AACR 2 rules. (The variety of problems from which to choose is nearly limitless, but space and time present their own limits.)

Two commentaries accompany the examples, one for the description and one for the choice and form of access points. These may be of use when you are interested in learning how we resolved a particular problem.

One observation about AACR 2 must be made here. The code no longer deals with the familiar 3 x 5 card format. It appears that the underlying principle of the new code is the concept of a single bibliographic record from which a variety of displays, in a number of different formats, may be created. Thus access points are considered of the same importance as the main entry heading, although for hardcopy (e.g., book or card, even microfilm) bibliographic formats the main entry heading still is an essential access point.

The choice and form of the access points are treated last. Referring to the examples, we compare the choice of main entry heading under the old and new rules. When these examples prove insufficient we occasionally illustrate a point by drawing on earlier cataloging. We take note of the decisions and options LC has chosen, since a large portion of that library's cataloging becomes part of our catalogs, particularly via the various bibliographic utilities. For those libraries having access to a utility's data base a knowledge of LC's options takes on even greater importance. A number of federal libraries are going to follow LC more closely—particularly since the Superintendent of Documents' catalogers are now receiving training by LC and will follow LC's options. Knowing these options will facilitate our decisions and anticipate some of the changes required to integrate new bibliographic records into our catalogs after Day 1.

One point must be remembered: no guide, manual or text can or should be a surrogate for the rules themselves. All of these are supplements, offering catalogers an opportunity to gain expertise and thereby to apply the new rules with greater ease. It is in this spirit that we prepared this text.

II

Glossary of Selected Terms and Acronyms

AACR 2 contains an excellent glossary which should be used in conjunction with this volume. The terms presented here include some new ones used in this work, some that presented problems of definition in discussions with colleagues, and some that are absent from the AACR 2 glossary. Readers are also advised to refer to Montague's excellent *Librarian's Glossary* (annotated in Chapter IX).

SELECTED TERMS

Access point. A collective term for any heading—either name or title or the main entry—which is entered in a catalog to provide access to an item.

Added entry. Any additional name, title or series title other than the main entry which can be used to identify and access an item.

Alternative title. A second title following the title proper, usually preceded by the conjunction "or." It generally is not a subtitle.

Area. The descriptive data on a bibliographic record consisting of one or more elements, e.g., title and statement of responsibility area; edition area; publication, distribution, etc. area.

Authorship. *See* Statement of responsibility.

Caption or **caption title.** A title printed at the beginning of an article, journal or other matter.

Chief source of information. The most preferred source of bibliographic data for the description of an item. It varies with type of material and is determined by the rules governing the material. *See also* Sources of information.

Collective title. The title proper given to a group of works issued in one publication.

Colophon. Publication and/or printing data given at the end of a book (see Example M21 in Chapter VI). It is not the publisher's identifying symbol or logo often found on the title page.

Corporate authors. *See* Corporate body.

Corporate body. An organization or group of individuals represented by a specific name. Included are associations, institutions, governments and their administrative units, etc. It supersedes the term "corporate author."

Element. A specific part of an area of description, or part of a name. For example, the edition statement is an element of the edition area, which may also include the statement of responsibility for the edition. For names, each component of a name is an element. It may also be a date, place or other qualifier.

Entry word. The first filing word of an entry or access point. Initial definite and indefinite articles are ignored.

Extent of item. An inclusive term relating to length of an item, in terms of pages, playing time, number of slides, etc. The specific material designation is included.

Filing title. *See* Uniform title.

Full stop. The British punctuation term for the American period (.).

Item. An inclusive term for any material, whether in printed or nonprint form, for which a bibliographic record is created.

Key title. A unique title given to a serial by the ISDS (International Serials Data System) at the time the ISSN (International Standard Serial Number) is assigned to an item.

Main entry. 1) The primary access point of a bibliographic record.
2) Conventionally, it also refers to the record which contains complete bibliographic data for an item, including tracings for added entries.

Multipart item. A collective term for items made up of several physical units—volumes of a book set, discs in an album, etc.

Other title information. A collective term for such data as subtitles, phrases indicating the content of an item, reasons for its publication, meeting data, etc. It is *not* the parallel title, spine title, running title, etc.

Personal author. The individual primarily responsible for the intellectual or artistic content of an item.

Preliminaries. The cover, title page, its verso and all pages, including their versos, preceding the title page.

Prominently named. Appearing in a formal statement in a prescribed source of information for the material to which it applies.

Running title. The title of a book or serial appearing at the top of each page and/or its verso.

Set. *See* Multipart item.

Sources of information. Sources of bibliographic data for the description of an item. They are outlined in the individual AACR 2 chapters for each format as the [Chapter X] ".0B" rules.

Stated prominently. *See* Prominently named.

Statement of responsibility. This term takes the place of "authorship." Like many of the AACR 2 terms, it is more inclusive and accommodates not only writers, but also artists, corporate bodies, performers and others responsible for the creation or presentation of the content of an item.

Subtitle. *See* Other title information.

Title. *See* Title proper.

Title proper. The name of an item, excluding subtitle and parallel title but including alternative title.

Uniform title. A standardized title by which a work has become known and under which variant forms of the title are cataloged in one file. Some titles are pure filing devices, used to group types of materials in one file.

UBC. Universal Bibliographic Control. A program of IFLA to make machine-readable bibliographic data universally available for all publications from and for all countries and to ensure that these data are compatible, correct and complete. The various ISBDs are products of UBC.

Utility. A service organization, such as OCLC, Inc., WLN and RLIN, which sells access to bibliographic data and products to libraries, either independently or brokered through a network. Subscribers may contribute their own data to the utility.

ACRONYMS

AACR 1	*Anglo-American Cataloguing Rules* (First Edition)
AACR 2	*Anglo-American Cataloguing Rules, Second Edition*
ALA	American Library Association
ANL	Australian National Library
ANSI	American National Standards Institute
BIP	Books In Print
CLA	Canadian Library Association
COM	Computer output microform
GMD	General material designation
GPO	Government Printing Office
IFLA	International Federation of Library Associations and Institutions
ISBD	International Standard Bibliographic Description
ISBD(G)	General International Standard Bibliographic Description: Annotated Text
ISBD(M)	International Standard Bibliographic Description for Monographic Publications
ISBD(NBM)	International Standard Bibliographic Description for Nonbook Materials
ISBD(PM)	International Standard Bibliographic Description for Printed Music (forthcoming)
ISBN	International Standard Book Number
ISDS	International Serials Data System
ISSN	International Standard Serial Number
LA	[British] Library Association
LC	Library of Congress
LCIB	*Library of Congress Information Bulletin*
JSCAACR	Joint Steering Committee for Revision of AACR
MARC	Machine-Readable Cataloging
NLC	National Library of Canada
OCLC	Now OCLC, Inc., formerly the Ohio College Library Center
PTLA	Publishers' Trade List Annual
RLIN	Research Libraries Information Network (formerly BALLOTS)
RTSD CCRC	Resources & Technical Services Division Catalog Code Revision Committee (ALA)
UBC	Universal Bibliographic Control
WLN	Washington Library Network

III

New Concepts in AACR 2

In terms of descriptive cataloging, "levels of description" and "optional rules" are the most important new concepts AACR 2 offers the librarian. With these, the quest for the bibliographic record that best serves the needs of a library user is furthered. AACR 2, with its three recommended levels of description and variety of options, allows a library to assess its users' bibliographic needs and to provide them with the most suitable record within the framework of the rules. Thus, if users can avail themselves of a new item as soon as possible after it has been acquired with the help of a brief—or level one—record, that record is sufficient.

DESCRIPTIVE LEVELS OF DETAIL

Considerations for Decisions

AACR 2 provides three levels of description: a first, or minimum level for an item, as defined in Rule 1.0D1; a second level, offering a somewhat fuller description (Rule 1.0D2); and a third and fullest level, including all the rules applicable to an item (Rule 1.0D3). The Library of Congress has indicated that it plans to establish its descriptive policies between the second and third levels,[1] and it is likely that other large research libraries will follow this example, although they may consider level one adequate for some of their material. Although this three-level concept is new to present-day catalogers, it was first stated informally by Cutter in 1904.[2] Librarians have, in fact, generally applied this theory, as evidenced by any catalog containing locally produced records.

Various factors must determine decisions on the fullness of bibliographic description: library priorities, the importance of an item to the collection and the item's relative value in the world of books. In addition, there are practical considerations, such as the volume of incoming material, the staff available to process newly acquired material and staff qualifications. At all times, the needs of the user should be part of the decision-making process, much of which should be based on simple good sense. As noted in Chapter I, the new rules require us to take a fresh look at our practices, to examine and record any changes when adopting AACR 2 and to follow these rules consistently—or at least until we decide to change them once again!

Levels of Description

The three levels of description require closer examination and analysis before we attempt to make decisions on how and where to apply them. They are not mutually exclusive; we are able to slide from one level to the other, with only the outer limits defined.[3] It is a mix-and-match environment for each format treated; we mix our levels of description to meet the format requirements for the item being cataloged (see Rule 0.29). The General Rules are further explained in Chapter IV.

In order to gain a better understanding of these three levels of description, we give two examples for each. These will be preceded by restating, from AACR 2, all those elements of description required for that particular level. We must keep in mind, however, that if the item does not contain the information defined by an element, then that element and its prescribed punctuation is not carried in the record (see Rule 1.0C, paragraph 5). These examples are followed by a decision table (Table III-4) at the end of this chapter, which gives the rules for each area of description and that area's elements. The table has been designed so that a library may record its decisions regarding a specific element in relation to a format (e.g., monograph, cartographic material).

First level

The first level of description requires as a minimum the following areas and their elements:

> Title proper / first statement of responsibility, if different from
> main entry heading in form or number or if there is no main entry
> heading. — Edition statement. — Material (or type of publication)
> specific details. — First publisher, etc., date of publication, etc. —
> Extent of item. — Note(s). — Standard number.

Following is an example for the first level of description, containing the statement of responsibility, which refers to the person or body responsible for the intellectual content of a work. Note that place of publication is *not* required for the first level. Figure III-1 is a facsimile of the title and copyright pages for this example. (Note that these pages do not provide all data necessary for even first level cataloging—e.g., number of pages.)

> *Example 1: 1st level of description*

> Health services planning / from the Department
>   of Community Medicine, St. Thomas' Hospital,
>   London. -- King Edward's Hospital Fund for
>   London, 1976.
>   55 p.
>   ISBN 0-900889-61-6.

Discussion

The title will be entered, according to Rule 21.1C (3), under its title with an added access point for the corporate body (see Rule 21.30E). The added entry is formulated by applying Rule 24.13, TYPE 1 and reads as follows: St. Thomas' Hospital (London). Department of Community Medicine.

Also note the changes in the capitalization and punctuation in the statement of responsibility. Appendix A (capitalization) Rules A.4H and A.18E require that the name of a corporate body be capitalized in the statement of responsibility. A period (full stop) was added to the abbreviation "St" according to American practice. The British practice is not to add a period to an abbreviation when the interior of a word is dropped—in this case, the "ain" in "Saint."

Example 2, below (see Figure III-2) has no statement of responsibility:

Example 2: 1st level of description

> Ascanius, or, The young adventurer. -- Garland,
> 1974.
>   64 p.
>   ISBN 0-8240-1116-3.

Discussion

The above example lacks the main entry heading, which would be: Burton, John, 1710-1771. The form of the author's name on the title page is identical to that of the main entry; consequently it does not have to be transcribed in a level one record (see Rule 1.0D1, explanatory information following the statement of responsibility element). This example is a facsimile edition of an early printed work; therefore Rule 1.11 (Facsimiles, Photocopies, and Other Reproductions), rather than Rules 2.12-2.18 (Early Printed Monographs), applies.

Second level

The second level of description requires, minimally, all the areas of description and their elements given below (Rule 1.0D2):

> Title proper [general material designation] = parallel title :
> other title information / first statement of responsibility ;
> each subsequent statement of responsibility. -- Edition
> statement / first statement of responsibility relating to the
> edition. -- Material (or type of publication) specific de-
> tails. -- First place of publication, etc. : first publisher,
> etc., date of publication, etc. -- Extent of item : other
> physical details ; dimensions. -- (Title proper of series /
> statement of responsibility relating to series, ISSN of series ;
> numbering within the series. Title of subseries, ISSN of
> subseries ; numbering within subseries).　　Note(s). -- ,
> Standard number.

Example 1: 2nd level of description (Refer to Figure III-1)

Health services planning [text] : a monograph /
    from the Department of Community Medicine, St.
    Thomas' Hospital, London ; edited by Karen
    Dunnell ; introd. by Walter W. Holland. --
    London : King Edward's Hospital Fund for London :
    Distributed for the King's Fund by Pitman Medical
    Pub. Co., 1976.
    55 p. : ill. ; 30 cm.
    References: p. 49-50.
    Includes index.
    ISBN 0-900889-61-6.

Discussion

With the addition of the editor's name in the subsequent statement of responsibility a second access point is gained under "Dunnell, Karen." Also note the expansion of the "publication, distribution, etc., area." The title, although published by a corporate body, is distributed by a trade publisher; therefore, the distributor was added in this example of a level two record. Rule 1.4B3, an all-inclusive rule, allows for the transcription of any places, names, and dates relating to publication and distribution.

Example 2: 2nd level of description (Refer to Figure III-2)

    Ascanius, or, The young adventurer [text] / John
Burton. -- New York : Garland, 1974.
    64 p. ; 19 cm. -- (The flowering of the novel)
    Attributed to John Burton. Cf. S. Haklett. Dict.
of anonymous and pseudonymous English literature.
    Originally published: London : Printed for G. Smith,
1741.
    ISBN 0-8240-1116-3.

Discussion

Compare the series information on the half-title page with its transcription in the series area. The series information is condensed to the series' title proper. The subtitle "Representative Mid-Eighteenth Century Fiction 1740-1775" and the other title information "A Collection of 121 Titles" were not added since the series title proper appeared to be distinctive without them (see Rule 1.6D1).

"A Garland Series" was interpreted as applying generally to the series statement and not as a specific second series statement.

Figure III-1: Title Page and Verso, Example 1

HEALTH SERVICES PLANNING

a monograph from the department of community medicine.
St. Thomas' Hospital, London

Edited by Karen Dunnell BSc(Soc)

Introduction by Professor Walter W. Holland, MD FRCP FSCM

Published by King Edward's Hospital Fund for London 1976

© King Edward's Hospital Fund for London 1976

Designed by Steve Storr

Typeset in Compugraphic Century Textbook

Printed in England by PPR Printing Limited, London

ISBN 0 900889 61 6

Distributed for the King's Fund by
Pitman Medical Publishing Company Ltd.

Figure III-2: Title Pages, Half-title Page, Verso, Example 2

Half-title page

Title page

A Garland Series

The
Flowering of the Novel

Representative Mid-Eighteenth
Century Fiction
1710-1775

A Collection of 121 Titles

Ascanius

Or, the Young Adventurer

John Burton

Garland Publishing Inc., New York & London

1974

Figure III-2 (Cont.)

Verso of title page   **Original title page**

Library of Congress Cataloging in Publication Data

Main entry under title:

Ascanius : or, The young adventurer.

   (The Flowering of the novel)
   Reprint of the 1746 ed., printed for G. Smith, London.
   1. Jacobite rebellion, 1745-1746--Fiction.
2. Charles Edward, the Young Pretender, 1720-1788--
Fiction.   I. Series.
PZ3.A7966 1974 [PR3291.A1] 823'.6   74-23693
ISBN 0-8240-1116-3

A S C A N I U S;

OR, THE

Young Adventurer,

A TRUE HISTORY.

*Tranflated from a Manufcript privately
banded about the Court of Verfailles.*

CONTAINING

A particular Account of all that happened
to a *certain* PERSON during his Wan-
derings in the *North,* from his memorable
Defeat in *April* 1746, to his final Efcape,
on the 19*th* of *September* in the fame Year.

———————

Ecce Homo !

———————

L O N D O N :

Printed for G. SMITH, near *Temple-Bar;* and fold
alfo by Meff. GRIMKY and VOGUEL, Bookfellers in *Amfterdam;* and by all other Bookfellers
in *Great-Britain, Ireland* and *Holland.*

Third level

In the third level of description all rules applicable to a physical medium may be applied to describe an item (see Rule 1.0D3).

Example 1: 3rd level of description (Refer to Figure III-1)

> Health services planning [text] : a monograph /
> from the Department of Community Medicine, St.
> Thomas' Hospital, London ; edited by Karen
> Dunnell ; introd. by Walter W. Holland. -- London :
> King Edward's Hospital Fund for London : Distributed
> for the King's Fund by Pitman Medical Pub. Co.,
> 1976.
> 55 p. : ill. ; 30 cm.
> The first paper Planning for health services, is a
> modification of the original German version which
> appeared in Handbuch der Sozialmedizin, vol. III, 1975.
> References: p. 49-50.
> Includes index.
> ISBN 0-900889-61-6

Discussion

To make the above example a third level of description record, we added an "Edition and history" note (Rule 1.7B7). The data in the note was taken from p. [3] of the preliminaries of the item.

Example 2: 3rd level of description (Refer to Figure III-2)

> Ascanius, or, The young adventurer [text] / John
> Burton. -- New York : Garland, 1974.
> 64 p. ; 19 cm. -- (The flowering of the novel)
> Attributed to John Burton. Cf. S. Haskell. Dict.
> of anonymous and pseudonymous English literature.
> Originally published: London : Printed by G. Smith, 1746.
> "... this facsimile has been made from a copy in the
> Beinecke Library Yale University (Col.pam.v.1036)."
> ISBN 0-8240-1116-3

Discussion

To make the above example of third level of description differ from the second level, we added a note giving the location of the original (see Rule 1.7B20).

Working in a Non-Network Environment

If the library in which you are working is independent from a network or machine-readable data base, you can make any decision you desire within the limits of your situation and the confines of the rules. As mentioned earlier, the purpose of your library and the type of service you are providing will probably be your first considerations. Some other aspects to be considered are available staff and its level of competence and experience.

With cataloging copy obtainable from various service agencies, it is doubtful that you will do original cataloging for all material received. But it is equally doubtful that your library will receive cataloging copy for all items acquired. Therefore, you may wish to follow the same level of description as your service agency for those formats for which you receive a high percentage of cataloging copy. For those formats for which only a small percentage of cataloging copy is available you may want to set your own level of description, which in turn depends on the importance of the format to your library's purpose.

The factors to be considered in your decisions are given in Table III-1.

Table III-1: Local Decision Factors for Bibliographic Formats: A Non-Network Environment

Extrinsic Factors	Intrinsic Factors
Staff-experience	Library's mission
Competence	Clientele served
Labor pool	Types of services provided
Cataloging copy services	Collection specialty
Formats for which copy is available	
Formats for which little copy is available	
Rule restrictions	

Working in a Network Environment

A network environment may place some constraints on a library's freedom to make decisions regarding levels of description. The decision may depend on which utility a network is brokering and whether several are brokered on the one a library chooses to join. The utilities—OCLC Inc., RLIN (Research Libraries Information Network) and WLN (Washington Library Network)—will also have to make decisions on minimum levels of description, choosing the first level or somewhere between the first and the second levels. Once the minimum standard for *National Level Bibliographic Record—Books* is published,[4] that standard could apply to all machine-readable data bases for the book format for the first-level bibliographic description.

When the utility from which a library receives its bibliographic data establishes a minimum level for description, librarians will have to incorporate that information in their decision-making process. Otherwise the same criteria apply as for independent libraries. The library's mission, the services supplied, the clientele served, the types of material acquired, collection specialties, staff available to process new material—all these must be considered in deciding on levels of description when working in a network environment.

Although the utility sets a minimum level of description for a format, a library would be required only to input new records at this level. If the utility's standard is above AACR 2's first level of description, a library is still free to opt for the code's first level. However, choosing a lower level than that required by a utility would be unwise economically. The library that makes such a choice would have to edit all records for a given format, if consistency is important. Thus it appears wise to have the local level of description for a particular format at least up to the standard required by the network or utility; a library may still select a higher level for any of the formats.

Table III-2 lists the factors to be considered in making decisions on the fullness of description for libraries working in a network environment.

Table III-2: Local Decision Factors for Bibliographic Formats: A Network Environment

Extrinsic Factors	Intrinsic Factors
Minimum levels	Library's mission
Set by a utility or	Clientele served
network	Types of services provided
Staff-experience	Collection specialty
Competence	
Labor pool	
Rule restrictions	

ADDITIONAL POINTS OF DECISION ON FULLNESS OF DESCRIPTION

In their introduction, the editors of AACR 2 launch the terms "alternative rules," "optional additions" and "optionally" into the regulated world of cataloging librarians. However, only "optional additions" and "optionally" are applied in Part I (Description). All three terms are employed in Part II (Headings, Uniform Titles, and References).

General Material Designation

One optional addition in AACR 2 is that of "General Material Designation" (GMD) (see Rule 1.1C). Rule 1.1C1 recommends two lists of GMDs, one for use by British agencies and the other for North American agencies (the latter list is more detailed). These designations describe the format of the item; "text," for example, applies to all printed material. Librarians will have to decide which GMDs to use because they supply significant additional information about the item; once a decision has been made it should be uniformly applied at that institution.

Let's take "microform," for example: its addition to the title quickly tells a user the item's format. This display may be very useful in a brief record in any register index catalog, either in COM or hard copy, in which only the main entry contains the full bibliographic data and all additional access points display a brief record, generally lacking the extent of item information. This same concept also applies to online circulation systems which may contain only the title and some basic imprint information. "Text" may be a designation of less value to many libraries.

Every format has an optional GMD, but a library may select its addition to only some of the formats. As a guide for your decisions, see LC's published choices for the GMD.*

---

*Cataloging Service Bulletin, No. 2, fall 1978; No. 6, fall 1979; and No. 8, spring 1980.

Optional Rules

Note that the General Rules in Chapter 1 of AACR 2 give optional additions to some rules. If the rule applies, the option can then be used with any other format. For example, in Chapter 5 (Music) Rule 5.1E1 states: "Record other title information as instructed in 1.1E." Rule 1.1E5 includes ". . . Optionally, add the other title information in other languages."

Optional rules can be divided into three categories:

1. Options given only as part of a general rule, and not repeated under specific formats, which apply to all formats if the rule applies. For example, Rule 1.4C7 states: "*Optionally,* add the full address of a publisher, distributor, etc. to the name of the place. Enclose such an addition in parentheses. Do not add the full address for major trade publishers."

2. Options repeated under each format if it is applicable, but sometimes with a slightly different number. For example, Rule 1.2B4 states: "*Optional addition.* If an item lacks an edition statement but is known to contain significant changes from previous editions, supply a suitable brief statement in the language and script of the title proper and enclose it in square brackets." In Chapter 9 (Machine-Readable Data Files) this rule is numbered 9.2B3 and has a slightly different wording: "*Optional addition.* If a machine-readable data file lacks an edition statement but is known to contain significant changes from previous editions, supply a suitable brief statement in the language and script of the title proper and enclose it in square brackets."

3. Options given only for the format to which it applies. For example, Rule 3.5D3 states: "For relief models, give the height x width in centimetres as instructed in 3.5D1, and *optionally* add the depth." This option would apply only to a relief model.

Since options add detail to the description, you must determine whether this level of fullness is required and serves a useful purpose in your library. Even if you decide to utilize some options for one format, you do not have to apply them to other formats. Certain formats may play a less important role in your library. Thus it may be necessary to decide item by item whether an option is to be applied, despite a general decision regarding the option.

TABLES FOR READY REFERENCE

Table III-3 lists Optional Rules, giving the various options preceded by the rule number and followed by the rule caption or brief text. The GMD is included in Table III-4 (the decision table for levels of descriptions), since it forms an integral part of a level, if it is added to your description. Again, you are referred to issues of the *Cataloging Service Bulletin* for LC's decisions on the options. Each table provides space for recording your own library's decisions and guidelines for application. These tables should be most helpful to librarians in a non-network environment, where there is greater latitude for local choice.

The Optional Rules Description Table

Table III-3 is a straightforward enumeration of all options for each format. "Analysis" has not been included since it does not contain options and is really description per se, applicable to any format.

The Decision Table for Levels of Descriptive Detail

The decision table is designed to aid in recording decisions for the more commonly found elements of description, or as a guide to developing local decision tables to accommodate local needs. The rules of Chapter 13 (Analysis) are not included since some are already covered under specific formats and others do not conform to the pattern set out in Chapters 1-12. These are "how-to" instructions like 1.9, 1.10 and 1.11 and not rules directly related to the levels of description.

If a rule is not applicable in level one or level two, "NR" (not required) is given under the respective format's chapter. If a rule is required, in any of the three levels, an "R" (required) is given at the coordinate of a chapter/format number and a rule. "NA" (not applicable) is recorded at the coordinate of a chapter/format number and the rule if the rule is not applicable. When the coordinate is blank, a local decision is required, and it can be recorded in that area.

The rule number column in this table uses "X" for all chapter numbers. The "X" is followed by the second level rule numbering. The second level rule numbering always refers to a specific area of description and is the same for each format; ".1", for example, is the "title and statement of responsibility" area for all formats. (This mnemonic scheme is further explained in the next chapter.) If an area is not used for a format, the rules themselves will indicate so by stating, for example, "This area is not used for printed monographs," as in Rule 2.3.

Although *all notes are optional,* they and the GMD have been made part of the table since they are included in the levels of description. All notes have been included, although they may not appear as part of every format or in the "General Rules." The captions for some of the notes change with a few formats but the concept treated remains the same; these differences are not indicated.

Table III-3: Optional Rules—Description

Rule No.	Rule Caption or Brief Text	Decision and Guidelines for Local Application (Fill in)
*1.1E5.	. . . *Optionally*, add the other title information in other languages.	
1.2B4.	*Optional addition*. If an item lacks an edition statement but is known to contain significant changes from previous edition, supply a suitable brief statement. . . .	
*1.4C7.	*Optionally*, add full address of a publisher. . . . Do not add the full address for a major trade publisher.	
	If this optional is chosen, Rule 1.4E1 must be used.	
1.4E	*Optional addition*. Statement of function of publisher, distributor, etc.	
*1.4F5.	*Optional addition*. Add the latest date of copyright following the publication . . . date if it is different.	
*1.4F8.	[For a multipart item published over a number of years] *Optionally*, when the item is complete, add the latest data.	
1.4G4.	*Optional addition*. Give the place, name of manufacturer and/or date of manufacture if they differ from the place, name of publisher . . . and are found in the item and are considered important. . . .	
*1.5A3.	. . . *Optionally*, make a note describing other formats in which they are available (see 1.7B16).	
*1.5B5.	[For multipart items not yet complete] *Optionally*, when the item is complete, add the number of physical units.	
1.5E1.	*Optional addition*. If method *d* is applicable and further physical description is desired add statement of extent, other physical details, and dimensions of the accompanying material as appropriate.	
1.8B2.	. . . *Optionally*, record more than one number and add qualification as prescribed in 1.8E. . . .	

*Precedes a general rule option when it applies to any format, although the option is not repeated under the format. For example, Rule 2.4C1 ("Record the place of publication, distribution, etc., as instructed in 1.4C.") is the only rule given for place of publication in Chapter 2 (Monographs).

Table III-3: Optional Rules—Description (Cont.)

Rule No.	Rule Caption or Brief Text	Decision and Guidelines for Local Application (Fill in)
1.8D.	*Optional addition.* Terms of availability. If the option is chosen Rule 1.8D1 applies.	
1.8E1.	Add after standard number or terms of availability . . . a brief qualification when an item bears two or more standard numbers and *optionally* when the terms of availability (See 1.8D) need qualification.	
2.2B3.	*Optional addition.* If an item lacks an edition statement but is known to contain significant changes from previous edition, supply a suitable brief statement. . . .	
2.4E.	*Optional addition.* Statement of function of distributor. If this option is chosen Rule 2.4E1 applies.	
2.4G2.	*Optional addition.* Give the place, name of prescriber, and/or date of printing, if they differ from the place, name of publisher . . . and are found in the item and are considered important.	
2.5E1.	Record the name, and *optionally*, the physical description, of a material that is issued with the item and is intended to be used in conjunction with it as instructed in 1.5E.	
2.8C.	*Optional addition.* Term of availability. If this option is chosen Rule 2.8C1 applies.	
2.8D2.	*Optional addition.* Record the type of binding as a qualification of the ISBN.	
2.16E.	If more than one place of publication, etc., is found in the item always record the first one and *optionally*, record the other statements. . . .	
2.16H.	*Optionally*, formalize the date if the statement appearing in the book is very long.	
2.17B.	*Illustrations.* . . . *Optionally*, add *woodcuts, metal cuts*, or in doubtful cases, *cuts*, as appropriate.	

Table III-3: Optional Rules—Description (Cont.)

Rule No.	Rule Caption or Brief Text	Decision and Guidelines for Local Application (Fill in)
2.18C.	Bibliographic references. For incunabula, and *optionally*, for other early printed monographs, give the place in standard lists where a description of the item being described is to be found.	
3.2B3.	*Optional addition.* If an item lacks an edition statement but it is known to contain significant changes from previous editions, supply a suitable brief statement. . . .	
3.3B2.	*Optional addition.* Give additional scale information that is found on the item.	
3.3C2.	*Optional addition.* Add associated phrases connected with the projection statement if they are found on the item. . . .	
3.3D.	*Optional addition.* Statements of coordinates and equinox. If this option is chosen 3.3D1 and 3.3D2 apply.	
3.4D1.	Record the name of the publishers, etc., and *optionally*, the distributor, as instructed in 1.4D.	
3.4E.	*Optional addition.* Statement of function of publisher and distributor, etc. If this option is chosen Rule 3.4E1 applies.	
3.4G2.	*Optional addition.* Give the place, name of printer, etc., and/or date of printing, etc., if they differ from the place, name of publisher, etc., . . .; and are found on the item, its container or case, or accompanying material. . . .	
3.5D1.	Maps, plans, etc. . . . *Optionally*, for early and manuscript cartographic items, give the dimensions to the nearest millimetre.	
3.5D3.	Relief models. For relief models, give height X width in centimetres as instructed in 3.5D1, and *optionally*, add the depth.	
3.5D5.	*Optional addition.* Containers. Add the dimensions of a container, specified as such, to the dimensions of the item.	

Table III-3: Optional Rules—Description (Cont.)

Rule No.	Rule Caption or Brief Text	Decision and Guidelines for Local Application (Fill in)
3.5E1.	Record the name and *optionally* the physical description of any material that is issued with the item and is intended to be used in conjunction with it, as instructed in 1.5E.	
3.8D.	*Optional addition.* Terms of availability. If this option is chosen Rule 3.8D1 applies.	
4.1F2.	*Optional addition.* If the name appended to, or the signature on, a manuscript is incomplete, add to it the name of the person concerned.	
4.4B1.	Give the date or inclusive dates of the manuscript or manuscript collection unless included in the title. . . . Give the date as year or years and *optionally* the month and day. . . , in that order.	
4.5B1.	Single manuscript. . . . *Optional addition.* Add, to the pagination, the number of leaves if this is different from the number of pages.	
4.5B2.	Collections of manuscripts. . . . *Optionally,* if the number of volumes or containers is recorded, add the number or approximate, number of items. . . . *Optionally,* add the number or approximate number of items or containers or volumes.	
4.5D2.	Collections of manuscripts. . . . *Optionally,* if the size is not uniform, give the size of the largest followed by *or smaller.*	
5.2B3.	*Optional addition.* If an item lacks an edition statement but is known to contain significant changes from previous editions supply a suitable brief statement. . . .	
5.4D1.	Record the name of the publisher, etc., and *optionally* the distributor, as instructed in 1.4D.	
5.4E.	*Optional addition.* Statement of function of publisher, distributor, etc. If this option is chosen Rule 5.4E1 applies.	

Table III-3: Optional Rules—Description (Cont.)

Rule No.	Rule Caption or Brief Text	Decision and Guidelines for Local Application (Fill in)
5.4G2.	*Optional addition.* Give the place, name of printer, and/or date of printing if they differ from place, name of publisher, distributor . . . and are found in the item and are considered important. . . .	
5.5E1.	Record the name, and *optionally* the physical description, of any material that is issued with the item and is intended to be used in conjunction with it. . . .	
5.8D.	*Optional addition.* Terms of availability. If this option is chosen Rule 5.8D1 applies.	
6.2B3.	*Optional addition.* If a sound recording lacks an edition statement but it is known to contain significant changes from previous editions, supply a suitable brief statement. . . .	
6.4D1.	Record the name of the publisher, etc., as instructed in 1.4D. *Optionally,* record the name of the distributor as instructed in 1.4D.	
6.4E.	*Optional addition.* Statement of function of publisher, distributor, etc. If this option is chosen Rule 6.4E1 applies.	
6.4G2.	*Optional addition.* Give the place, name of manufacturer, and/or date of manufacture if they differ from the place, name of publisher. . . and are found in the item and are considered important. . . .	
6.5B1.	Record the number of physical units of a sound recording by giving the number of parts in arabic numerals and one of the following terms as appropriate: . . . . *Optionally,* if general material designations are used and the general material designation includes the word *sound,* drop the word *sound* from all of the above terms except the last.	
6.5C8.	*Optional addition.* Recording and reproduction characteristics. For sound recording, give the recording and reproduction characteristics.	

Table III-3: Optional Rules—Description (Cont.)

Rule No.	Rule Caption or Brief Text	Decision and Guidelines for Local Application (Fill in)
6.5E1.	Record the name, and *optionally* the physical description, of any accompanying materials as instructed in 1.5E.	
6.8D.	*Optional addition.* Terms of availability. If the option is chosen Rule 6.5D1. applies.	
7.1B2.	[If an item lacks a title, supply one as instructed in 1.1B7. and also follow these particular instructions.]	
	Optionally, give a description of the action and length of each shot in a note (see 7.7B18).	
7.2B3.	*Optional addition.* If a motion picture or video recording lacks an edition statement but is known to contain significant changes from previous editions, supply a suitable brief statement. . . .	
7.4E.	*Optional addition.* Statement of function of publisher, distributor, etc. If this option is chosen 7.4E1 applies.	
7.4F2.	*Optionally*, give a date of original production differing from the date of publication, distribution, etc., in the note (see 7.7B9).	
7.4G2.	*Optional addition.* Give the place, name of manufacturer, and/or date of manufacture if they differ from the place, name of publisher . . . and are found in the item and are considered important. . . .	
7.5B1.	Record number of physical units of a motion picture or video recording. . . . *Optionally*, if general material designations are used and the general material designation indicates that the item is a motion picture or video recording, drop film or video from all the above items.	
7.5E1.	Record the name, and *optionally* the physical description, of any accompanying material as instructed in 1.5E.	
7.8D.	*Optional addition.* Terms of availability. If this option is chosen Rule 7.8D1 applies.	

Table III-3: Optional Rules—Description (Cont.)

Rule No.	Rule Caption or Brief Text	Decision and Guidelines for Local Application (Fill in)
8.2B3.	*Optional addition.* If a graphic item lacks an edition statement but is known to contain significant changes from previous editions, supply a suitable brief statement. . . .	
8.4E.	*Optional addition.* Statement of function of publisher, distributor, etc. If this option is chosen Rule 8.4E1 applies.	
8.4G2.	*Optional addition.* Give the place of manufacture, name of manufacturer, and/or date of manufacture if they differ from the place and name of publisher . . . and are found on the item and are considered important. . . .	
8.5B1.	[Extent of item] Record the number of physical units of a graphic item. . . . *Optionally,* substitute or add a term more specific than those listed above.	
8.5C7.	Photographs . . . *Optionally,* give the process used.	
8.5E1.	Record the name, and *optionally* the physical description of any accompanying material as instructed in 1.5E. . . .	
8.8D.	*Optional addition.* Terms of availability. If this option is chosen Rule 8.8D1 applies.	
9.2B3.	*Optional addition.* If a machine-readable data file lacks an edition statement but is known to contain significant changes from the previous edition, supply a suitable brief statement. . . .	
9.4E.	*Optional addition.* Statement of function of publisher, producer, distributor, etc. If this option is chosen Rule 9.4E1 applies.	
9.5D1.	[accompanying material] Record the designation for a program accompanying a data file. . . . *Optionally,* add to the designation the number of statements or logical records in such accompanying programs or files.	

Table III-3: Optional Rules—Description (Cont.)

Rule No.	Rule Caption or Brief Text	Decision and Guidelines for Local Application (Fill in)
9.7B4.	Variations in title. . . . *Optionally*, record a data set name differing from title proper.	
9.8D.	*Optional addition*. Terms of availability. If this option is chosen Rule 9.8D1 applies.	
10.2B3.	*Optional addition*. If an item lacks an edition statement but is known to contain significant changes from previous editions, supply a suitable brief statement.	
10.4E.	*Optional addition*. Statement of function of publisher, distributor, etc. If this option is chosen Rule 10.4E1 applies.	
10.4G3.	*Optional addition*. Give the place, name of manufacturer, and/or date of manufacture if they differ from the place, name of publisher . . . and are found on the item or accompanying textual material or on a container and are considered important. . . .	
10.5B1.	[Extent of item] *Optionally*, if general material designation are used and the general material designation consists of one of the above listed terms, drop that term and give the number of copies only.	
10.5B2.	Add to the designation . . . the number and the name(s) of the pieces. If the pieces cannot be named concisely or cannot be ascertained, add the term *various pieces*, and *optionally* give the details of the pieces in a note (see 10.7B10).	
10.5E1.	Record the name, and *optionally* the physical description, of any accompanying material as instructed in 1.5 E.	
10.8D.	*Optional addition*. Terms of availability. If this option is chosen Rule 10.8D1 applies.	
11.2B3.	*Optional addition*. If a microform lacks an edition statement but is known to contain significant changes from previous editions, supply a suitable brief statement. . . .	

Table III-3: Optional Rules—Description (Cont.)

Rule No.	Rule Caption or Brief Text	Decision and Guidelines for Local Application (Fill in)
11.4E.	*Optional addition.* Statement of function of publisher, distributor, etc. If this option is chosen Rule 11.4E1 applies.	
11.5B1.	[Extent of item] Record the number of physical units of a microform item by giving the number of parts in arabic numerals. . . . *Optionally,* if the general material designation *microform* is used, drop the prefix *micro* from these terms.	
11.5E1.	[Accompanying material] Record the name, and *optionally* the physical description, of any accompanying material as instructed in 1.5E.	
11.7B10.	Physical description. . . . *Film. Optionally,* give details of the nature of the film used.	
11.8D.	*Optional addition.* Terms of availability. If this option is chosen Rule 11.8D1 applies.	
12.2B3.	If an edition statement appears in two or more languages or scripts, give the statement that is in the language or script of the title proper . . . and *optionally,* the parallel statement(s), each preceded by equal signs.	
12.4E.	*Optional addition.* Statement of publisher, distributor, etc. If this option is chosen Rule 12.4E1 applies.	
12.4G2.	*Optional addition.* Give the place of manufacture, name of manufacturer, and/or date of manufacture if they differ from the place and name of publisher . . . and are found in the serial and are considered important.	
12.5E1.	[Accompanying materials] Record the name, and *optionally* the physical description, of any material that is intended to be used in conjunction with the serial, as instructed in 1.5E. . . .	

Table III-3: Optional Rules—Description (Cont.)

Rule No.	Rule Caption or Brief Text	Decision and Guidelines for Local Application (Fill in)
12.7B7e.	[Relationship with other serials] *Split.* If a serial is the result of the split of a previous serial into two or more parts, give the name of the serial that has been split, and *optionally* the name(s) of other serial(s) resulting from the split.	
12.7B7f.	[Relationship with other serials] *Absorption.* If [a] serial is absorbed by another serial, give the name of the serial absorbed and *optionally* the date of absorption. . . . If a serial is absorbed by another serial, give the name of the serial, give the name of the absorbing serial, and *optionally* the date of absorption.	
12.8D.	*Optional addition.* Terms of availability. If this option is chosen Rule 12.8D1 applies.	
12.8E1.	[Qualification] *Optional addition.* Add qualification to terms of availability as instructed in 1.8E.	

Table III-4: Decision Table for Levels of Descriptive Detail

Rule No.	1st level	2nd Level	3rd Level	2 Monograph	3 Cartographic	4 Manuscript	5 Music	6 Sound Record.	7 Motion Pict. / Videorecords.	8 Graphic Mat.	9 Machine-Read. Data File	10 3-Dimensional Artifacts, etc.	11 Microforms	12 Serials
x.1B	Title proper	Title proper	Title proper	R	R	R	R	R	R	R	R	R	R	R
x.1C	NR	[General material designation] optional element	Same as 2nd level	—	—	—	—	—	—	—	—	—	—	—
x.1D	NR	Parallel title	Same as 2nd level	—	—	—	—	—	—	—	—	—	—	—
x.1E	NR	Other title information	Same as 2nd level	—	—	—	—	—	—	—	—	—	—	—
x.1F	Statement of responsibility [give first statement only and give it only if it is not the same in form and number as the main entry]	Statements of responsibility	Same as 2nd level	R	R	R	R	R	R	R	R	R	R	R
x.2B	Edition statement	Same as 1st level	Same as 1st level	R	R	R	R	R	R	R	R	R	R	R
x.2C	NR	First statement of responsibility relating to the edition	Same as 2nd level	—	—	—	—	—	—	—	—	—	—	—
x.2D	NR	NR	Subsequent edition statements	—	—	—	—	—	—	—	—	—	—	—
x.2E	NR	NR	Statements of responsibility relating to subsequent editions	—	—	—	—	—	—	—	—	—	—	—
x.3	Material (or type of publication) specific details	Same as 1st level	Same as 1st level	NA	R	NA	NA	NA	NA	NA	NA	NA	R	R

Key:

NR = Not required   R = Required   NA = Not applicable   —— = Fill in your library's decision

Table III-4: Decision Table for Levels of Descriptive Detail (Cont.)

Rule No.	1st level	2nd Level	3rd Level	Monograph 2	Cartographic 3	Manuscript 4	Music 5	Sound Record. 6	Motion Pict. Videorecords. 7	Graphic Mat. 8	Machine-Read. Data File 9	3-Dimensional Artifacts, etc. 10	Microforms, etc. 11	Serials 12
x.4C	NR	*First* place of publication, specific details	Place of publication, distribution, etc.											
x.4D	Name of publisher, distributor, etc.	*First* publisher, etc.	Name of publisher, distributor, etc.	R	R	NA	R	R	R	R	R	R	R	R
x.4F	Date of publication	Same as 1st level	Same as 1st level	R	R	NA	R	R	R	R	R	R	R	R
x.4G	NR	NR	Place of manufacture, name of manufacturer, date of manufacture			NA								
x.5B	Extent of item (including specific material designation)	Same as 1st level	Same as 1st level	R	R	R	R	R	R	R	R	R	R	R
x.5C	NR	Other physical details	Same as 2nd level											
x.5D	NR	Dimensions	Same as 2nd level											
x.5E	NR	NR	Accompanying material											
x.6B	NR	Title proper of series statement	Same as 2nd level											
x.6C	NR	NR	Parallel title of series											
x.6D	NR	NR	Other title information of series											
x.6E	NR	Statement of responsibility relating to a series	Same as 2nd level											

Table III-4: Decision Table for Levels of Descriptive Detail (Cont.)

Rule No.	1st level	2nd Level	3rd Level	2 Monograph	3 Cartographic	4 Manuscript	5 Music	6 Sound Record.	7 Motion Pict. Videorecords.	8 Graphic Mat.	9 Machine-Read. Data File	10 3-Dimensional Artifacts, etc.	11 Microforms	12 Serials
x.6F	NR	ISSN of series	Same as 2nd level											
x.6G	NR	Numbering within series	Same as 2nd level											
x.6H	NR	Title of subseries, ISSN of subseries, numbering within subseries	Title of subseries, parallel title of subseries, statement of responsibility relating to subseries, ISSN of subseries, numbering within subseries											
x.6J	NR	More than one series statement	Same as 2nd level											
x.7B...	Notes — all notes are optional	Same as 1st level	Same as 1st level											
x.7B1	Nature, scope or artistic form of the item	Same as 1st level	Same as 1st level									NA		
x.7B2	Language of the item and/or translation or adaption	Same as 1st level	Same as 1st level											
x.7B3	Source of title proper	Same as 1st level	Same as 1st level											
x.7B4	Variations in title	Same as 1st level	Same as 1st level											
X.7B5	Parallel titles and other title information	Same as 1st level	Same as 1st level											
x.7B6	Statements of responsibility	Same as 1st level	Same as 1st level											

Table III-4: Decision Table for Levels of Descriptive Detail (Cont.)

Rule No.	1st level	2nd Level	3rd Level	2 Monograph	3 Cartographic	4 Manuscript	5 Music	6 Sound Record.	7 Motion Pict./Videorecords.	8 Graphic Mat.	9 Machine-Read. Data File	10 3-Dimensional Artifacts, etc.	11 Microforms	12 Serials
x.7B7	Edition and history	Same as 1st level	Same as 1st level					NA						
x.7B8	Material specific details	Same as 1st level	Same as 1st level					NA	NA			R	NA	
x.7B9	Publication, distribution, etc.	Same as 1st level	Same as 1st level											
x.7B10	Physical description	Same as 1st level	Same as 1st level											
x.7B11	Accompanying materials and supplements	Same as 1st level	Same as 1st level											
x.7B12	Series	Same as 1st level	Same as 1st level			NA								
x.7B13	Dissertations	Same as 1st level	Same as 1st level									R		NA
x.7B14	Audience	Same as 1st level	Same as 1st level											
x.7B15	Reference to published descriptions	Same as 1st level	Same as 1st level		NA	NA	NA	NA	NA	NA		NA	NA	NA
x.7B16	Other formats available	Same as 1st level	Same as 1st level		NA	NA	NA					NA	NA	
x.7B17	Summary	Same as 1st level	Same as 1st level		NA	NA	NA							
x.7B18	Contents	Same as 1st level	Same as 1st level											

Table III-4: Decision Table for Levels of Descriptive Detail (Cont.)

Rule No.	1st level	2nd Level	3rd Level	2 Monograph	3 Cartographic	4 Manuscript	5 Music	6 Sound Record.	7 Motion Pict. Videorecords.	8 Graphic Mat.	9 Machine-Read. Data File.	10 3-Dimensional Artifacts, etc.	11 Microforms	12 Serials
x.7B19	Numbers borne by the item (other than those covered by .8)	Same as 1st level	Same as 1st level			NA								
x.7B20	Copy being described and library's holdings	Same as 1st level	Same as 1st level			NA					NA			
x.7B21	"With" notes	Same as 1st level	Same as 1st level			NA				NA	NA	NA		
x.7B22	Ancient medieval and Renaissance manuscripts	Same as 1st level	Same as 1st level	NA	NA		NA	NA	NA	NA	NA	NA	NA	
x.8B	Standard ISBN, ISSN	Key-title	Same as 1st level	R	R	NA	R	R	R	R	R	R	R	R
x.8C	NR	Terms of availability	Same as 2nd level	NA	NA	NA	NA	NA	NA	NA	NA	NA	NA	R
x.8D	NR	Terms of availability	Same as 2nd level											
x.8E	NR	Qualifications	Same as 2nd level											

IV

Applying the General Rules for Description

GENERAL RULES AND INDIVIDUAL FORMATS

The arrangement of areas of description in Chapter 1 of AACR 2, General Rules for Description, sets the pattern for each of the individual formats in following chapters. As stated earlier, and as shown in the decision tables in Chapter III of this guide, the first level in the rule numbering scheme refers to a chapter/format. Thus, each chapter number, except 1 and 13, stands for a format. Chapter 3 refers to cartographic materials, for example, and Chapter 5 to music. Although AACR 2 treats "analysis" separately in Chapter 13, the rules set forth there are in effect general rules also. Chapter 13, like Chapter 1, applies to all formats.

As stated in Rule 13.1, "Scope":

> . . . Some of the methods of analysis are related to
> provisions found in other chapters, but all the
> methods are collected here with general guidelines
> to assist in the selection of one of the means of
> analysis.

A library, and you as a librarian, must establish a policy for this set of "guidelines," a term more apt than "rules" in the case of Chapter 13.

HOW THE RULES ARE CONSTRUCTED

Before we continue with the details of the rule structure and how these in turn relate to the individual formats, an overall view of their construction is appropriate. A vertical mock-up will highlight each component of the rule construction; "N" represents a number and "A" an alpha (or letter).

Rule N.NAN

N - Chapter number/specific format
. - Period (full stop) separates chapter and rule
N - Second number representing area of description or rule
A - Alpha representing rule information applicable to the area of description or an element of the area
N - Third numeric representing specific problem or characteristic of an element of the area

This is the simple, recurring pattern of numbering in the chapters of description. The mnemonic aspect of this scheme surpasses AACR 1 by far in ease of use; AACR 1 is simply a sequential string of rules lacking a system. With this scheme in mind, we can now begin with the analysis of the rule structure.

The first set of rules in each chapter is the .0 group. Under .0, the rules supply general rules, those which apply to the description of the format in toto, and also set the parameters for the material in a given format. These individual subsets in the .0 group are:

.0A Scope
.0B Source of information
.0C Punctuation
.0D Level of details in the description
.0E Language and script of the description
.0F Inaccuracies
.0G Accents and other diacritical marks
.0H Items with several title pages or several chief sources of information
.0I Description of whole or part [Chapter 3 only]

Each format has its own set of .0 rules. Essentially the information is repetitive; yet there are instances in which variations are given which apply only to that chapter's format. When the text of these rules is identical to those in Chapter 1 or any other chapter, only a simple reference to the pertinent rule is given. For example, Chapter 12 (Serials) includes the following instructions:

12.0B2. Sources of information. Nonprinted serials
Follow the instructions given at the beginning of the relevant chapter in Part I (e.g., for sources of information for a serial sound recording, see Chapter 6).

or

12.0C. Punctuation
For the punctuation of the description as a whole see 1.0C.
For prescribed punctuation of elements, see the following rules.

It must be noted here that Chapter 1 is slightly different from the other chapters on description for subrules .0A and .0B. Here, 1.0A deals with "sources of information," and is subdivided into two aspects—general concepts for selecting sources of information and the treatment of items lacking a chief source of information. Rule 1.0B defines the organization of description and enumerates the areas of description. Although this last subrule is not repeated in any of the chapters which deal with a specific format, it determines the breakdown of the rules for this and the remaining chapters. "1.0A. Sources of information" drops to x.0B in the succeeding chapters, and "Scope" takes up the position of .0A.

Description follows the established conventions. The basic eight areas of description are listed in Table IV-1.

Table IV-1: Basic Areas of Description as Defined by AACR 1 and AACR 2

AACR 2 Terminology	AACR 2 Subrule No.	AACR 1 Terminology
Title and statement of responsibility	.1	Title and author statement
Edition	.2	Same
Material (or type of publication) Specific detail [used for cartographic material and serials only]	.3	Holdings (serials); no designation for maps, etc.
Publication, distribution, etc.	.4	Imprint
Physical description	.5	Collation
Series	.6	Same
Note(s)	.7	Same
Standard number and terms of availability	.8	ISBN (Chpt. rev only)

A quick examination of the terminology used for the rules of .1 and .3-.5 reveals a broadening of the concepts from AACR 1 to cover any format now in existence or developed in the future. The terms that stayed the same already had broader meanings and are applicable to any format. The ISBN area has been broadened to include ISSNs and any other standard numbers that may be developed.

Other rules, however, go beyond treating the various areas of description; they also address specific cataloging problems: supplementary items (.9); items made up of several types of materials, e.g., kits (.10); facsimiles (.11). And in Chapter 2 (books, etc.), Rules 2.12-2.18 treat early printed monographs. With these few exceptions the rules are built very systematically and the pattern of description, as outlined above, can be transferred from the first chapter, General Rules, to all succeeding chapters on description. Although the chapter number changes, the second level of rule numbering remains constant and is transferable across the formats.

A very similar scheme is applied to the third and fourth levels of the numbering system for each area of description. Alphas are used to label the different elements of an area. Complex elements are subdivided numerically, with each subdivision treating a specific characteristic or problem; however, they do not cover all problems encountered in cataloging an item, as the examples in Chapter VI of this guide illustrate. Analogous to the .0 rules, which apply to the format as a whole, the "A" in the third level of rule numbering applies to the area of description as a whole and nearly always deals with its prescribed punctuation. The "B" rules relate to the first element of an area and the "C" rules to the next one, etc. Each numeric which follows the "B" rule then addresses a specific aspect or problem of the element. Visualization of this concept will be easier when we examine the following outline of second and third level rule numbering:

.xA   Prescribed rule
.xA1 Punctuation
.xB   Area of description—1st element
.xB1 Rule and application
.xB2 Each subsequent number (e.g., .xB3, etc.) treats a specific characteristic or problem of the element
.xC   Second element
.xC1 Rule governing element
.xC2 Each subsequent number (.xC3 etc.) treats another characteristic or problem of the element
.xD, .xE, etc. New element or variant

Not all elements have a subset of numbers to treat special characteristics or problems, and if an area consists of only one element, only an .xA and .xB will occur. There are always an .xA and .xB for each area. A good example is the note area; each note has only one element, the note itself, so that the note rule number for any format never goes beyond .xB. However, since there are many types of notes (22 to be exact), this area has the greatest number of third level rule subsets.

If we want to apply the rules of description effectively, we must keep this scheme in mind. Once the changes in Chapter 1 have been mastered the rules under the individual formats or types of publications are quite easily applied.

SOURCES OF INFORMATION FOR DESCRIPTION

The development of the ISBD (International Standard Bibliographic Description) and the publication of the ISBD for monographs* gave impetus to a more precise definition and systematic approach to sources of information for description. The principles employed for all formats are drawn together in ISBD(G)** and state that:

1. ". . . the information found on the item itself normally is preferred to information found elsewhere";
2. there is a preferred order of sources;
3. each area of description has its own principal sources of information.[1]

---

*ISBD(M): *International Standard Bibliographic Description for Monographic Publication* (preliminary edition, 1971; first standard edition, 1974; revised first standard edition, 1978).

**ISBD(G): *General International Standard Bibliographic Description: Annotated Text,* 1977.

The 1974 revisions of Chapter 6, "Separately Published Monographs," of AACR 1 already reflected these changes. AACR 2 applies the principles to all its formats, another feature which should allow a librarian to move from format to format with greater ease. The item itself always remains the chief source of information; however, the importance of the title page or its equivalent, in relation to square bracketed data in the description, has been limited to the title and statement of responsibility.

AACR 2 breaks down sources of information into two categories—the chief sources of information and prescribed sources of information. "Chief sources of information" guides the librarian in selecting that source which will provide the required data in a complex situation and supplies substitutes when the chief source is lacking.

In AACR 2 these guidelines are always found under Rule .0B1 of each of the chapters. A simplified, more schematic, approach in presenting these appears in ISBD (M) and ISBD (S).[2] In systematizing these guidelines for the four examples in Table IV-2, the same approach was taken. The choices for selecting the sources is given in descending order, starting with the preferred one.

Table IV-2: Chief Sources of Information for Description

Monographs

1. Title page or its substitute
2. Part of item supplying most information, in this order: cover (but *not* dust jacket), half title page, caption, colophon, running title or another part
3. Any available source, including reference sources and publishers' catalogs

Music

1. Title page or the "list" title page, if title being cataloged is included, or a title page substitute
2. Part of item supplying most information, in this order: cover (but *not* dust jacket), half title page, caption, colophon, running title or another part
3. Any available source, including reference sources and publishers' catalogs

Microforms

1. Title frame, should bear the full title and publication data
2. Rest of the item (including container when it is an integral part)
3. Container
4. Accompanying eye-readable material
5. Any other source

Serials

1. Title page or a title page substitute of *first* issue
2. First issue available
3. In order of preference:
   cover, caption, masthead, editorial page, colophon, other pages

While the chief source of information rules guide you in the selection of cataloging data, the prescribed sources set the requirements for selection and punctuation. AACR 2, like AACR 1 and the 1949 *Green Book* (LC's rules for description) still make it an ironclad rule that data transcribed from a source outside of the prescribed one must be placed in square brackets ([ ]). The prescribed sources and the chief source of information may be the same; however, only for the title and statement of responsibility area is the prescribed source limited to the chief source of information.

For the other areas (i.e., other than title and statement of responsibility) the information required to describe an item may be taken from a variety of sources. There is no real pattern, but there is a general scheme for all formats. To visualize this scheme, Table IV-3 matches the areas of description with their sources of information. We must remember, however, that individual formats have their own requirements and that the chief source of information will differ with each format; for example, a monograph will always have the title page as its chief source of information.

Table IV-3: Areas of Description: Generalized Sources of Information

Area of Description	Prescribed Source of Information
Title and statement of responsibilities	Chief source
Edition	Chief source and format variants
Material specific details	Chief source and format variants
Publication, distribution, etc.	Chief source and format variants
Physical description	Item itself or any source (format dependent)
Series	Chief source and format variants
Notes	Any source
Standard number and terms of availability	Any source

V

Punctuation

Under AACR 1 and previous rules, libraries employed conventional punctuation and spacing. The results were as nonstandard as in other forms of communication. This diversity was compounded by some libraries, which single-spaced after a period (full stop) in order to save a few spaces on the 3 x 5 card.

With the publication of Chapter 6, revised, of AACR 1, conventional punctuation gave way to prescribed punctuation. The impetus for the change was the development of the ISBDs, which prescribed punctuation and spacing for bibliographic description. The new rules were devised to facilitate the interchangeability of bibliographic records among various national agencies, to assist in the interpretation of records across language barriers, and to ease the conversion of records to machine-readable form.[1] The three examples below will make the point. (Note the use of an *en* dash for the *em* dash in AACR 2.)

Dutch (Flemish) : *Bibliographie de Belgique*
Sybesma-Knol, Neri. -
Bibliographie van het nieuwe zeerecht : 2 = Bibliography
on the new law of the sea. - 1050 Brussel (Pleinlaan 2) :
Centrum voor de studies van het recht van Verenigde naties
en van de gespecialiseerde organisaties, 1977. - 188 p.

French: *Bibliographie de Belgique*
Stander Bernd. -
La vente à tempérament et son financement dans le Marché
Commun : 3 : le droit allemand.   5000 Namur (Rampart
de la Vierge 5) : Société d'études morales, sociales
et juridiques, 1977. - 435 p. - (Travaux de la
Faculté de droit de Namur ; 5). - 1.350 F

German: *Deutsche Bibliographie*
Prunkl, Gottfried: Josip Broz-Tito : in Selbstzeugnissen
u. Bilddokumenten / dargest. von Gottfried Prunkl u.
Axel Rühle. [Den Anh. besorgten d. Autoren]. - 14. - 16.
Tsd. -- Reinbeck bei Hamburg : Rowholt, 1979. - 155 S. :
ill.; 19 cm. - (Rowholts Monographien ; 109) □ Bibliogr. J.

Broz-Tito u. Literaturverz. S. 147 - 153. - Nebent. :
Tito / Gottfried Prunkl ; Axel Rühle. ISBN 3-499-50 199-6
kart. : Dm 6.80.

PRESCRIBED PUNCTUATION: AACR 2

AACR 2 treats the general mechanics of prescribed punctuation in Chapter 1, General Rules, and discusses them in some detail. Once the punctuation as a vehicle for identifying data has been mastered, anyone can glean the pertinent data needed to identify the bibliographic item and acquire it. The pattern is simple. Each area is preceded by a period-space-dash-space (. --), unless the area begins a new paragraph (in which case there is no preceding punctuation). Even the German record, with its slight variations, can easily be analyzed. The notes, employing prescribed punctuation as recommended by AACR 2 and ISBD(M), should not present a problem either.

There are eight areas of description, each with its own elements. If an item does not have the data defined by the element, the element and its preceding punctuation are not represented in the record. There is one exception, however: the "Publication, distribution, etc., area." Data lacking here must be so specified (see Rules 1.4C6, 1.4D5 and 1.4F7).

Chapter III in this guide listed all areas of description and nearly all the elements of each area. They will be presented here once again, this time in outline form and preceded by or enclosed in their punctuation, as appropriate.

    I. Title and statement of responsibility, etc., area
    [no preceding punctuation]
            Title proper
            [General material designation]
     = Parallel title
     : Other title information
     / Statement of responsibility
     ; Subsequent statements of responsibility

   II. Edition area
     . -- Edition statement
     / Statement of responsibility relating to the edition
     , Subsequent edition statement
     / Statements of responsibility relating to
        the subsequent edition statement

 III. Material (or type of publication) specific details area
    Chapter 3. Cartographic materials -- mathematical data area
     . -- Statement of scale
     ; Projection statement
        (Statement of coordinates and equinox)

    Chapter 12. Serials -- numeric and/or alphabetic
          chronological, or other designation area

. -- Numerical and/or alphabetical designation
   or
. -- Chronological designation
  (Chronological designation after numbering)
= More than one numbering system
; New sequence of numbering, for successive designations

IV. Publication, distribution, etc., area
 . -- Place of publication, distribution, etc.
 , Subsequent place of publication, distribution, etc.
 : Publisher, distributor, etc.; repeat for each
  publisher, distributor, etc. given
 , Date of publication, distribution, etc.
  (Place of manufacture : name of manufacturer,
  date of manufacture)

V. Physical description area
 . -- Extent of item (including specific material designation)
 : Other physical details
 ; Dimensions
 + Accompanying material

VI. Series area
 . -- (Title proper of series
 = Parallel title of series
 : Other title information of series
 / Statement of responsibility relating to series
 , ISSN
 ; Numbering within series
 . Subseries)
(Note that parentheses surround the total series statement.)

VII. Note area
(The note area either begins a new paragraph or is also preceded by a
period-space-dash-space (. --). For internal punctuation see Rules 1.7A1
and 1.7A3.)

VIII. Standard number and terms of availability area
 . -- Standard number [*Omit* preceding punctuation when beginning a
  new paragraph.]
 = Key-title
 : Terms of availability
  (qualifications)
 . -- Subsequent standard number

  The interpretation of bibliographic information in languages not using the Roman
alphabet but employing prescribed punctuation is facilitated because the sequence of each

area and its elements is fixed, and each element in an area can be identified by its preceding punctuation. In other words, punctuation acts as a code. The period (full stop) space-dash-space preceding all areas, except the first, can be seen as a signal announcing new data.

The internal punctuation for notes follows the prescribed punctuation whenever the data presented correspond to the order of the area and the elements of description (see Rule 1.7A3, "Form of notes"). The only exception is the period (full stop) space-dash-space (. --) which is replaced by a simple period. Punctuation is repeated with each format and element of an area.

Since the punctuation is systematic and logically applied, the following table (V-1) showing its patterns may aid in the application. The table is preceded by an index to facilitate its use. The index lists the punctuation mark which must precede each element of description. The punctuation marks are arranged according to the alphabetical sequence of the element terms. Indexing is for both pre-AACR 2 and AACR 2 terminology. You can, for example, find the slash mark (/) preceding "statement of responsibility" (AACR 2) and also preceding "author statement" (pre-AACR 2).

INDEX TO PUNCTUATION TABLE

Punctuation Mark		Term or Element
+		accompanying material
(	)	address of publisher, distributor, etc.
=		alternative numbering
,		alternative title
. --		areas of description (except first one)
/		author statement
;		author statement, secondary
* ?		conjectural data *(follows the data)
(	)	coordinates and equinox, statement of
;		coordinates, cartographic material
,		dates
		publishing, distribution, etc.
		manufacturing
		printing
;		dimensions
:		distributor's name
=		edition statement, parallel in two or more languages
. --		edition statement
,		edition statement, second
. . .		ellipses
;		equinox, cartographic material
[	]	general material designation
-		holdings, inclusive
:		ill.

[ ]		s. l. (sine loco)
[ ]		s. n. (sine nomine)
/		statement of responsibility
		title
		edition
		series
		notes
:		subsequent name of publisher, distributor
;		subsequent place of publishing, distribution
;		subsequent statements of responsibility in edition area
		notes
		series
		title
.		subseries, title
:		subtitle
		series title
		title proper
.		supplement
		series
		title
[ ]		supplied data
		pagination
		volume designations, etc.
[ ]		symbols, description of
:		terms of availability
;		titles proper in collection without collective title
;		volume designation in series

Table V-1: Punctuation

Application/Description	Space	No Space	Pre-punc.*	No Space	Space

COLON: Space-colon-space
Precedes all other title information and each subsequent other title information (e.g., Notes on the progress of the colored people of Maryland since the war : a supplement to The Negro in Maryland : a study of the institution of slavery 1). This applies also to other title information given in series statements and informal notes.
Precedes in 1. Publication, distribution, etc., area
      a. The name of the publisher, distributor, etc.
      b. All subsequently named publishers, distributors, etc.
      c. Manufacturer's name.
    2. Physical description area, the physical details (e.g., ill.).
    3. Standard number and the terms of availability.
	X		:		X

No space-colon-space *Follows* the introductory wording of a formal note in the note area (e.g., Contents: . . .; Rev. of: . . .)		X	:		X
COMMA: No space-comma-space *Follows* the title proper and *precedes* the alternative title in the title and statement of responsibility area (e.g., Ascanius, or, The young adventurer), and in a formal note. *Precedes* a subsequent edition statement in the edition area (e.g., 2nd ed., printed with additions). *Precedes* all dates in the publication, distribution, etc. area, even such dates which have been supplied and enclosed in square brackets, e.g., [1979?]. *Precedes* the ISSN of a series or subseries.		X	,		X
DASH: No space-dash (or two hypens)–no space *Separates* "each longitude or latitude from its counterpart" (see AACR 2 Rule 3.3D1).		X	--	X	

*Pre-punc. = prescribed punctuation.

Table V-1: Punctuation (Cont.)

Application/Description	Space	No Space	Pre. punc.*	No Space	Space
EQUAL SIGN: Space-equal sign-space *Precedes* each parallel title which may include other title information and the statement of responsibility in all areas of description. *Precedes* a parallel edition statement in two or more languages. *Precedes* alternative numbering in the numeric and/or alphanumeric . . . designation area.	X		=		X
FULL STOP (PERIOD): No space-full stop (period)-dash (two hyphens)-space *Precedes* each new area of description, except the first or those areas which begin a new paragraph.		X	. --		X
No space-full stop (period)-two spaces		X	.		XX
Precedes in 1. Title and statement of responsibility area, the title of a supplementary item or section which is not grammatically linked to the title proper (see AACR 2 Rule 1.1B9). 2. Series area, the title of the subseries.					
HYPHEN: No space-hyphen-no space Generally use the hyphen to indicate continuity or inclusiveness, i.e., v. 1-4, or v. 1- , or 1964-1968, or 1980- , etc. Its most common usage is in the following areas: 1. Numeric and/or alphabetic . . . designation area -- place a hyphen after the first numeric and/or alphabetic serial designation and/or the first date. Follow it *either* by four spaces, if the item is continuing, or by the same data for the last issue if or when the item ceases publication. 2. Publication, distribution, etc. area--place a hyphen after the date of the first item published in a multipart item. Follow it either by four spaces or the date of the last published item/part.		X	-	X	

Table V-1: Punctuation (Cont.)

Application/Description	No Space	Space	Pre. punc.*	No Space	Space
OMISSION MARKS: Space-omission marks-space *Insert* for data omitted when the title proper, and/or other title information and/or the statement of responsibility is shortened (see AACR 2 Rules 1.1B4, 1.1E3 and 1.1F5).		X	. . .		X
PARENTHESES: Space-set of parentheses-space *Place* the following elements in parentheses: 1. Statement of coordinates in the mathematical area for cartographic material (AACR 2 Rule 3.3D). 2. Date (month, year) following the numeric serial volume designation. 3. Publisher's, distributor's, etc. address. 4. Place, name and date of manufacture, when applicable. 5. Physical description area data which adds specificity to an element of an area (see individual AACR 2 rules), such as continuous paging for a set of volumes, number of components after the extent of the item (e.g., playing time), or colored illustration data or "the physical details of accompanying materials." 6. Note area—the physical details in a formal note which follows prescribed punctuation. (This is not specifically stated in the rules but consistently applied in the examples.)		X	( )		X
PLUS SIGN: Space-plus sign-space *Precedes* accompanying materials data recorded in the physical description area.		X	+		X
QUESTION MARK: No space-question mark-no space *Add* to conjectural information, particularly the publication date (enclose data in square brackets since it is not taken from a prescribed source of information).	X		?	X	
SEMICOLON: Space-semicolon-space *Precedes* each subsequent statement of responsibility in any area of description, including formal notes.		X	;		X

Table V-1: Punctuation (Cont.)

Application/Description	Space	No Space	Pre. punc.*	No Space	Space

Precedes each title proper of a collection of works by one author lacking a collective title and without one predominant part or section.
Precedes each subsequent place of publication, distribution, etc.
Precedes in 1. Physical description, the dimensions (e.g., size).
    2. Series area, the volume designation or series enumeration.
    3. Numeric and/or alphabetic . . . designation area, each new sequence of numbering (see AACR 2 Rule 12.3G).
    4. Mathematical data area (cartographic material), the equinox statement.					

SLASH: Space-slash-space *Precedes* all statements of responsibility in any area of description, including those in formal notes.	x		/		x
No space-slash-no space *Separates* latitude and longitude in the mathematical area for cartographic material.		x	/	x	
SQUARE BRACKETS: Space-set of square brackets-space *Place* in square brackets ([ ]) all interpolated descriptive data; the square brackets are preceded and followed by a space. *Enclose* interpolated elements of one area when they follow one another in one set of brackets. Interpolated elements following one another but belonging to different areas of description are each enclosed in a pair of square brackets and separated from one another by the prescribed punctuation, the full stop (period)-space-dash-space (. --). This includes 1. "Sic" for misspellings or inaccuracies transcribed from the prescribed source of information. 2. Cataloger's description of symbols not reproducible with available typographic	x		[ ]		x

Table V-1: Punctuation (Cont.)

Application/Description	Space	No Space	Pre. punc.*	No Space	Space
facilities (e.g., partial derivative of *u* with respect to *x*).					
3. Any general material designation (GMD).					
4. "S.l." and/or "s.n."					
5. Supplied: dates					
last page number not given in the item, or other pages or leaf numbering					
numeric, alphabetic, chronologic or other serial volume designation.					

PUNCTUATION PROBLEMS

A few special problems are noted below. Punctuation changes in the transcription of titles (Rule 1.1B1):

Change ". . ." (ellipses points) to "--" (dash) and
    "[ ]" (square brackets) to "( )" (parentheses)
if they are part of the title proper. (The dash is not surrounded with spaces.)

Double punctuation:

1) If the end punctuation of an element transcribed from its chief source of information is retained, the prescribed punctuation with its proper spacing must also be added.
Example: Who's minding the children? : the history & politics of day care in America.

Go to bed! : a book of bedtime poems.
2) If an abbreviation is placed in square brackets, the standard punctuation preceding the following element must be added.
Example: . -- [Hamburg] : Springer, [1961?]. -- (Mathematische Sammlungen)

. -- Wahoo, Neb. : [s.n.], 1975

Omitting punctuation:

Drop the period (full stop) from the period space-dash-space (. --) if it follows an abbreviation.

Example: . -- 2nd ed. -- London : IFLA International
            Office for UBC, . . .
         . -- xlix, 165 24 p. : ill. ; 25 cm. -- (Special . . .
A second period (.) was not added to "ed." and "cm."

Square brackets problems:

More than one element is enclosed in square brackets only if they are part of one area.

VI

Description:
Cataloging Examples, Old and New

The previous three chapters discussed the major new concepts and changes of description in AACR 2. Chapter III examined levels of descriptive detail and the decisions we must make to apply the new rules effectively. Two decisions are necessary: (1) which level of detail should be used to describe each bibliographic unit in a given format, and (2) which optional rules should be applied or not applied to that specific format. Chapter IV discussed how the general rules work and how they interact with the format-specific rules of the various chapters in AACR 2. Chapter V dealt with the prescribed punctuation.

These three areas can be seen as the grid which must be constructed before concrete can be poured to shape a structure—to give and maintain its form.

Now, following the sequence of AACR 2—describing an item before determining the choice and form of access points—we will bibliographically describe a variety of items in selected formats. The emphasis is on monographs, but serials, microforms, music and sound recordings are also treated. As previously noted, once description per se is understood, cataloging in any format will become less difficult. Under the new rules there are fewer exceptions by type of material; the difficulty lies primarily in breaking some old habits and traditions.

HOW THE EXAMPLES ARE CONSTRUCTED

Each example presented in this chapter has an alphanumeric (letter/number) identifier followed by a descriptive title. The title gives the format (e.g., Sound Recording) and then a descriptive phrase about the type of item and/or problem, in the following manner:

Example SR1 (Sound Recording): Collection with Collective Title and a Single Performer

We then show the AACR 2 bibliographic example, followed by a pre-AACR 2 record. The latter is generally the record produced at the time the item was first issued, and we indicate whether or not this record is LC copy. Subsequently, under the heading "Discussion," each descriptive area is commented upon and similarities or differences between AACR 1 and

AACR 2 are pointed out. (An area will only be discussed when it represents a change in the rules.) Generally, the text of the rules is not quoted but a reference to the appropriate rule is made. However, when it appears useful to illuminate a statement or an example, a partial quote from the rule may be given.

Access points in the AACR 2 form are also given in the examples. In some instances there are few or no changes from the pre-AACR 2 form, particularly when the rules of AACR 1, Chapter 6, revised, were applied. (That record often was already in the AACR 2 form.) The examples are nearly all given in the third and fullest descriptive level. It would seem more beneficial to present the maximum record, in order to provide a basis for the selection of levels of description.

AACR 2 does not address itself to the format a bibliographic record should or may take, or how to paragraph, if that is the form chosen. Punctuation "precedes" and does not follow an area. Therefore, we had to arrive at our own format for the examples and make some decisions on punctuation. We decided to end each paragraph with a period (full stop), as this has been the general convention. This reflects our decision on the examples' format: paragraphing with a two-space indentation. The first paragraph includes: (1) title and statement of responsibility area; (2) edition area; (3) material (or type of publication) specific details area; and (4) publication, distribution, etc., area.

The second paragraph consists of the physical description and the series area. Each note is treated, as in the past, like a single paragraph. The main entry heading begins at the left margin, and the title and statement of responsibility area begins the first paragraph below it. The title main entry also begins at the left margin, but each line in the first paragraph is indented two spaces (see Example M8); thus we continued with the traditional form of the hanging indentation.

Access points naturally fall into two groups: main entry and added entries. When there is a change, the new rule is discussed and, when appropriate, the old rule may be referred to.

Although the choice of access points and their forms are dealt with in detail in subsequent chapters, a few comments must be made. The initials in personal names were filled out and added in parentheses—e.g., Bell, D.A. (David Arthur)—when the full form was given in the pre-AACR 2 record and only the initials appeared on the title page. This suggests a means of integrating the new heading for a personal name with the old one. Note that LC has chosen to apply the option of stating the full given names ". . . whenever the information is readily available"[1] (also see Rule 22.16A). It appears economical to anticipate this and so be able to merge LC cataloging copy with our own records.

We also chose, for the same reason, to add the data or dates to the name when these were available (see Rule 22.18).[2] However, LC's options were not chosen for the music examples because the composers are better known without their full names (e.g., Edward MacDowell, rather than Edward Alexander MacDowell in Example MU2). The dates appeared superfluous and were also omitted.

Before we deal with a selected number of formats it may be advantageous to restate briefly the purpose of the discussion. It is a practical one; we are trying to demonstrate how to resolve problems by applying the existing rules and by working within the framework of the code.

MONOGRAPHS

Monographs is one of two formats which arrived at its new AACR 2 form in a two-step process; nearly all the changes occurred in AACR 1, Chapter 6, revised, issued in 1974. (The other format is audiovisual media and special instructional materials, Chapter 12, revised in 1975.) In AACR 2, monographs are treated in Chapter 2 (Books, Pamphlets, and Printed Sheets). It must be noted that the new rules require more knowledge about books, their make-up and patterns of publication; they omit the explanatory remarks of the functions of some areas of description given in AACR 1 and its revised Chapter 6. Examples here would be the edition area (compare AACR 1 Rule 135; Chapter 6, revised, rule 135; and AACR 2 Rules 1.2B and 2.2B) and the imprint area (compare AACR 1 Rule 138; Chapter 6, revised, Rule 136; and AACR 2 Rules 1.4B1 and 2.4B).

Although most of the changes have been in effect since 1974, we will nevertheless comment briefly on some of them. We are attempting here to aid catalogers whose professional experience predates the 1974 change and those who have only cataloged with rules influenced by the ISBD (M).

Title and Statement of Responsibility

Starting with the first area, title and statement of responsibility, the AACR 2 rules continue to keep the author's name in the title when "it is an integral part of the title proper" (Rule 1.1B2). Otherwise the statement of responsibility is transcribed following the title proper or other title information, as required by the chief source of information, the title page. Thus the statement of responsibility for author or publisher will be present in most records, since we may no longer omit it when it is in the main entry heading (see Example M2). In AACR 2 only the first level of description permits the omission of the statement of responsibility, but it must be identical to the main entry heading.

Totally new in AACR 2 is the GMD (general material designation). This element is optional but we added it to all examples, in all four formats, to illustrate its use. Each library will of course make its own decision on whether or not to include it; the Library of Congress' decision not to use the designation "[text]" is perfectly acceptable.

Another change is that a parallel title may now be followed by its statement of responsibility; this is a change in AACR 2 not already present in AACR 1, Chapter 6, revised. Whether to transcribe the parallel title and also its statement of responsibility depends upon the level of description selected by your library or cataloging department.

Edition Area

As noted earlier, the new rules are more prescriptive and detailed in some cases, e.g., the edition area. The rules give precise instructions on how to transcribe and punctuate the statement of responsibility in this area. They also differentiate between a primary edition statement and a subsequent edition statement (see Example M3 and Rule 2.2D1). The subsequent edition statement rule (2.2D1) is new, although a hint of it appears in Rule 135A of the revised Chapter 6.

Publication, Distribution, etc.

In the publication, distribution, etc. area, no other substantive changes between the 1974 revision and AACR 2 have occurred, but there have been several changes from the original rules. To indicate a lacking place of publication we no longer give the abbreviation "[n.p.]" for "no place" (of publication). Instead, we use a Latin abbreviation which will be the same in all countries using ISBD (M) bibliographic description. The new abbreviation is "[S.l.]" (*sine loco*, meaning "without place"); it is also given in square brackets but the "s" is capitalized since it begins a new area. (Note that there is no space between the letters.) Since the 1974 revision more than one place of publication is transcribed when one of the place names, in a secondary position, is located in the country of the cataloging agency (Rule 1.4B8).

There has been one rule reversal. AACR 1, Chapter 6, revised, requires that the original publisher's information, covered by a label which gives different imprint data, be transcribed "if legible" (Rule 136A). With AACR 2 we again transcribe the data on the label (see Rules 1.4B6 and 2.4B), and the original publication information is given again in the note.

The new rules also require, as previously noted, that the publisher's name be transcribed even when it is also the main entry. The original rules permitted the omission of this data when it was identical to the main entry. This change was made in the 1974 revision. However, the name may be abbreviated (see Example M20). It is now possible to add a minor publisher's address (see Rule 1.4C7 and Example M12). In the examples we considered a publisher to be a major trade publisher if listed in PTLA (*Publishers' Trade List Annual*) or BIP (*Books In Print*) or their foreign equivalents. Example M11, for instance, gives the address of the Council of Europe's U.S. distributor since the distributor's name could not be found in these sources.

Publication dates will continue to be a problem in certain instances and will depend on the interpretation an individual library makes. We refer to reissues of a title with an edition-type statement that often indicates only a reprinting, as occurs with foreign language titles. The addition of the distribution date (see Rule 1.4F4) will also require a ruling by a library.

Physical Description

The physical description area also contains some changes. One is that the ampersand (&) preceding the accompanying material data has been replaced by a plus (+), as shown in Examples M20-M23. There have been a number of changes in recording pagination; Hagler's *Where's That Rule?* (see Chapter IX) has discussed these in some detail. But you should be aware of another reversal. The AACR 1, Chapter 6, revised, Rule 141B3c required that "loose-leaf" information be given in a note; now it is once again, as in the original AACR 1 Rule 142B2, part of the physical description (collation) (Rule 2.5B9), as in "1 v. (loose-leaf)." Finally, AACR 2 continues the details for leaves or pages of plates but some of the illustration designations have changed or been deleted. "Charts" has been added, "diagrams" and "graphs" deleted and "portraits" now applies to both individual and group portraits.

Series Area

The series rules underwent additional changes which enhanced the interpretation of the data in this area. No longer do "His," "Her," "Its" or "Their" precede the title and refer to the main entry. Instead this area follows the general rules and sequence of description—title proper : other title information / statement of responsibility. Thus the author follows the title proper and never precedes it unless the name is part of the series title proper (see Example M15). The series statement of Example M6 could read:

> (Studies in income and wealth / by the Conference
> on Research in Income and Wealth ; v. 32)

had we not decided that the series title was distinctive and did not need a statement of responsibility to differentiate it from another title.

With AACR 2 the "generic" title concept presented in Chapter 6, revised, Rule 142E3 has been dropped, but the problem that led to its introduction has not been resolved. Library of Congress and National Library of Canada have worked on another concept, that of the "unique title," for series and serials with identical titles. We can assume that if this concept is adopted by the Joint Steering Committee for the Revision of AACR (JSC), a rule addition will be published.

Another change in this area is the position of the ISSN (see Examples M18 and S8). The ISSN had formerly been tagged onto the series after the volume numbering; now it is linked to the series title to which it was assigned.

Notes

The rules on notes have also been revised and are a distinct improvement. The order of the notes, as we have previously mentioned, follows the same sequence as the areas of description to which they refer. Only two types of notes precede; the first deals with the "Nature, scope, or artistic form of the item" and the other with the "Language of the item and/or translation or adaptation." Another simplification occurred with "Bound with" (volumes issued separately but bound together at a later date) and "Issued with" data (two titles, each with its own title page but published together in one volume). We no longer differentiate between these two forms and record the data after a simple "With:".

The ISBN treatment has been expanded. Besides the number and a specific volume qualifier, we may now add the price and binding information. More than one ISBN may also be given (see Example M2).

One additional change must be noted. Supplements or supplementary material are either treated as accompanying material or are cataloged as separate items; the "dashed on" entry has disappeared.

These appear to be the major changes AACR 2 has wrought in the monograph format. There are, of course, others. Some may be illustrated in the examples, as are some of the difficulties.

EXAMPLE M1

Title Page of Vol. 1

THE JOURNALS AND
LETTERS OF
FANNY BURNEY
(MADAME D'ARBLAY)

◈

VOLUME I · 1791–1792
LETTERS 1-39

◈

Edited by
JOYCE HEMLOW
with
CURTIS D. CECIL
and
ALTHEA DOUGLAS

OXFORD
AT THE CLARENDON PRESS
1972

Title Page of Vol. 6

THE JOURNALS AND
LETTERS OF
FANNY BURNEY
(MADAME D'ARBLAY)

◈

VOLUME VI
FRANCE 1803–1812
LETTERS 550-631

◈

Edited by
JOYCE HEMLOW
with
GEORGE G. FALLE, ALTHEA DOUGLAS
and
JILL A. BOURDAIS DE CHARBONNIÈRE

OXFORD
AT THE CLARENDON PRESS
1975

Oxford University Press, Ely House, London W. 1

GLASGOW NEW YORK TORONTO MELBOURNE WELLINGTON
CAPE TOWN IBADAN NAIROBI DAR ES SALAAM LUSAKA ADDIS ABABA
DELHI BOMBAY CALCUTTA MADRAS KARACHI LAHORE DACCA
KUALA LUMPUR SINGAPORE HONG KONG TOKYO

ISBN 0 19 812516 X

© Oxford University Press 1975

Verso of Vol. 6 Title Page

EXAMPLE M2

Title Page

PLAYSCRIPT 45

'a macbeth'
FREELY ADAPTED FROM
SHAKESPEARE'S TRAGEDY

charles
marowitz

CALDER AND BOYARS · LONDON

Verso of Title Page

First published in Great Britain 1971 by
Calder and Boyars Limited
18 Brewer Street, London W1R 4AS

© Charles Marowitz 1971

The photographs in this volume are by John Haynes
and may not be reproduced without permission.

© John Haynes 1971

All performing rights in this adaptation are strictly
reserved and applications for performances should be
made to
Charles Marowitz, Open Space Theatre,
32 Tottenham Court Rd., London W.1.

No performance of the adaptation may be given unless
a licence has been obtained prior to rehearsal.

ISBN 0 7145 0719 9 Cloth Edition
ISBN 0 7145 0720 2 Paper Edition

Printed by photo-lithography
and made in Great Britain at
The Pitman Press, Bath.

Title Page

ANATOMY,

DESCRIPTIVE AND SURGICAL.

BY

HENRY GRAY, F.R.S.,

FELLOW OF THE ROYAL COLLEGE OF SURGEONS AND LECTURER ON
ANATOMY AT ST. GEORGE'S HOSPITAL MEDICAL SCHOOL.

WITH FIVE HUNDRED AND TWENTY-TWO ENGRAVINGS ON WOOD.

THE DRAWINGS BY H. V. CARTER, M.D., AND DR. WESTMACOTT.

THE DISSECTIONS JOINTLY BY THE AUTHOR AND DR. CARTER.

WITH AN INTRODUCTION ON GENERAL ANATOMY AND DEVELOPMENT.

BY

T. HOLMES, M.A. CANTAB.,

SURGEON TO ST. GEORGE'S HOSPITAL; MEM. CORRESP. DE LA SOC. DE CHIR. DE PARIS.

A NEW AMERICAN

FROM THE

EIGHTH AND ENLARGED ENGLISH EDITION.

TO WHICH IS ADDED

LANDMARKS, MEDICAL AND SURGICAL.

BY LUTHER HOLDEN, F.R.C.S.,
SURGEON TO ST. BARTHOLOMEW'S AND THE FOUNDLING HOSPITALS.

PHILADELPHIA:
HENRY C. LEA.
1878.

EXAMPLE M4

Title Page

Verso of Title Page

Made in the United States of America
Reprinted 1975

Library of Congress Cataloging in Publication Data

Adams, Frank Dennette, 1892-
   Adams' Physical diagnosis.

   First-11th ed. by R. C. Cabot (1st-2d ed., with
title: Physical diagnosis of diseases of the chest);
12th-13th ed. by R. C. Cabot and F. D. Adams; 14th
ed. by F. D. Adams.
   1. Physical diagnosis. I. Burnside, John W., ed.
II. Cabot, Richard Clarke, 1868-1939. Physical
diagnosis of diseases of the chest. III. Title.
IV. Title: Physical diagnosis. [DNLM: 1. Diagnosis.
WB200 A212p 1974]
RC76.A3 1974   616.07'54   74-862
ISBN 0-683-00038-1

Composed and printed at the
Waverly Press, Inc.
Mt. Royal and Guilford Aves.
Baltimore, Md. 21202, U.S.A.

Adams'
Physical Diagnosis

An Introduction to Clinical Medicine

FIFTEENTH EDITION

John W. Burnside, M.D.

Chief, Division of Internal Medicine,
The Milton S. Hershey Medical Center of
the Pennsylvania State University

The Williams & Wilkins Company/Baltimore

EXAMPLE M5

Half-title Page

Aktuelle Probleme in der Psychiatrie
Neurologie/Neurochirurgie

HERAUSGEGEBEN VON
PROFESSOR DR. P. KIELHOLZ, BASEL
PROFESSOR DR. H. KAESER, BASEL
PROFESSOR DR. M. KLINGLER, BASEL

BAND 5

Die Entstehung der Schizophrenie
The Origin of Schizophrenia

HERAUSGEGEBEN VON / EDITED BY
M. BLEULER UND J. ANGST

Title Page

Die Entstehung der
Schizophrenie

The Origin of Schizophrenia

HERAUSGEGEBEN VON / EDITED BY
M. BLEULER UND J. ANGST

UNTER MITARBEIT VON
J. ANGST
S. ARIETI
G. BENEDETTI
M. BLEULER
E. KRINGLEN
J. LUTZ
D. ROSENTHAL
J. SHIELDS

VERLAG HANS HUBER BERN STUTTGART WIEN

SYMPOSIUM
zum 100jährigen Bestehen der
Psychiatrischen Universitätsklinik Burghölzli-Zürich
und zu Ehren von Professor Dr. MANFRED BLEULER
(am 3./4. Juli 1970 in Zürich).

Library of Congress Catalog Card Number: 78-148114

Verso of Title Page

64

EXAMPLE M6

Half-title Page

NATIONAL BUREAU OF ECONOMIC RESEARCH
CONFERENCE ON RESEARCH IN INCOME AND WEALTH

Title Page

*The Industrial Composition
of Income and Product*

JOHN W. KENDRICK, *editor*
THE GEORGE WASHINGTON UNIVERSITY

Studies in Income and Wealth
VOLUME THIRTY-TWO
*by the Conference
on Research in Income
and Wealth*

NBER

NATIONAL BUREAU OF ECONOMIC RESEARCH
NEW YORK

Distributed by COLUMBIA UNIVERSITY PRESS
NEW YORK AND LONDON 1968

Verso of Title Page

Relation of National Bureau Directors to
Publications Reporting Conference Proceedings

Since the present volume is a record of conference
proceedings, it has been exempted from the rules
governing submission of manuscripts to, and crit-
ical review by, the Board of Directors of the
National Bureau. It has, however, been reviewed
and accepted for publication by the Director of
Research.

*Resolution adopted July 6, 1948,
as revised November 21, 1949*

EXAMPLE M7

Title Page

Glaucoma Update

International Glaucoma Symposium
Nara/Japan, May 7–11, 1978

Editors

G. K. Krieglstein and W. Leydhecker

With 48 Figures

Springer-Verlag Berlin Heidelberg New York 1979

Verso of Title Page

Library of Congress Cataloging in Publication Data
International Glaucoma Symposium, Nara, Japan, 1978.
Glaucoma update.

Bibliography: p. Includes index.
1. Glaucoma-Congresses. 2. Glaucoma in children-
Congresses. I. Krieglstein, G. K. II. Leydhecker, Wolfgang.
III. Title. [DNLM: 1. Glaucoma-Congresses.
W3 IN1244 1978r / WW290 I59 1978r]
RE871.I53 1978 617.7'41 79-10747

ISBN 3-540-09350-8 Springer-Verlag Berlin Heidelberg New York
ISBN 0-387-09350-8 Springer-Verlag New York Heidelberg Berlin

Printed in Germany.

The use of registered names, trademarks, etc. in this publication does not imply,
even in the absence of a specific statement, that such names are exempt from the
relevant protective laws and regulations and therefore free for general use.

Offsetprinting and bookbinding: Konrad Triltsch, Würzburg

2127/3020—543210

EXAMPLE M8

Title Page

A Guide to Planning and Conducting
Environmental Study Area Workshops

developed cooperatively by
National Education Association

and

National Park Service
U.S. Department of the Interior

National Education Association
Washington, D.C. 20036

Verso of Title Page

This material prepared for the National Park Service,
U.S. Department of the Interior; published 1972.
Library of Congress Catalog Card Number 72-83859
NEA Stock No. 381-11998

EXAMPLE M9

Half-title Page

WILEY SERIES ON PERSONALITY PROCESSES

IRVING B. WEINER, *Editor*
Case Western Reserve University

Interaction in Families
by Elliot G. Mis
Social Status an
by Bruce P. Do
Psychological D
by Irving B. We
Assessment of
by Elbert W. Ru
Black and White
by Stuart Hause
The Humanizat
by Robert I. Ha
and Lois Blackw
Adolescent Sui
by Jerry Jacobs
Toward the Inte
by John M. Reis
Minimal Brain
by Paul Wender
Structure and F
by Eric Klinger
LSD: Personalit
by Harriet Linto
Leo Goldberger
Treatment of th
by James F. Ma
Psychopatholog
edited by Murie
Abnormal Child
by Anthony Dav
Principles of Ps
by John M. Reis
Aversive Mater
by Alfred B. Hil
Individual Diffe
edited by Jack C
Ego Functions
Diagnostic, and
by Leopold Bell
Innovative Trea
edited by Karen

Title Page

UNDERSTANDING
THE RAPE VICTIM
A Synthesis of Research Findings

SEDELLE KATZ

MARY ANN MAZUR, M.D.
Department of Psychiatry
Washington University
School of Medicine

A WILEY-INTERSCIENCE PUBLICATION

JOHN WILEY & SONS, New York ● Chichester ● Brisbane ● Toronto

Verso of Title Page

Library of Congress Cataloging in Publication Data

Katz, Sedelle, 1923-
  Understanding the rape victim.

  (Wiley series on personality processes)
  "A Wiley-Interscience publication."
  Bibliography: p.
  Includes index.
  1. Rape. 2. Victims of crimes. 3. Sex
crimes. 1. Mazur, Mary Ann, 1946-   joint
author. II. Title.
HV6558.K37   362.8'8   78-25704
ISBN 0-471-03573-4   ●

Printed in the United States of America
10 9 8 7 6 5 4 3 2 1

Title Page

Poverty Amid Plenty

The American Paradox

The Report of The President's Commission on Income Maintenance Programs November 1969

Publication Data from Preliminary Pages

For sale by the Superintendent of Documents, U.S. Government Printing Office
Washington, D.C. 20402 - Price $1.75 (paper copy)

iv

EXAMPLE M11

Title Page

COUNCIL OF EUROPE

———

EUROPEAN PUBLIC HEALTH COMMITTEE
CO-ORDINATED MEDICAL RESEARCH
(1974 Programme)

MIDWIVES IN EUROPE
PRESENT AND FUTURE
EDUCATION AND ROLE OF THE MIDWIFE
IN COUNCIL OF EUROPE MEMBER STATES
AND IN FINLAND

REPORT

prepared by Mr J.M.L. PHAFF (Netherlands)
Mrs L. SASSI (Italy)
Mrs L. VALVANNE (Finland)
presented by Professor E.J. HICKL (Fed. Rep. of Germany)
Director of Studies

STRASBOURG 1975

Verso of Title Page

Title Page
J. Burke Severs Editor

© 1972 by The Connecticut Academy of Arts and Sciences

ISBN 0-208-01220-6
Library of Congress catalog card number 67-7687
Printed in the United States of America

J. BURKE SEVERS
GENERAL EDITOR

A Manual of the Writings in Middle English

1050-1500

*By Members of the Middle English Group of the
Modern Language Association
of America*

Based upon
A Manual of the Writings in Middle English 1050-1400
by John Edwin Wells, New Haven, 1916
and Supplements 1-9, 1919-1951

ALBERT E. HARTUNG
GENERAL EDITOR

A Manual of the Writings in Middle English

1050-1500

*By Members of the Middle English Group of the
Modern Language Association
of America*

Based upon
A Manual of the Writings in Middle English 1050-1400
by John Edwin Wells, New Haven, 1916
and Supplements 1-9, 1919-1951

THE CONNECTICUT ACADEMY OF ARTS AND SCIENCES
MDCCCCLXX

Order from

ARCHON BOOKS
The Shoe String Press, Inc.
995 Sherman Ave.
Hamden, Connecticut 06514

THE CONNECTICUT ACADEMY OF ARTS AND SCIENCES, NEW HAVEN, CONNECTICUT
MDCCCCLXXII

Title Page
Albert E. Hartung Editor

Verso of Title Page

EXAMPLE M13

Title Page

Title Page

Developmental
Programming
for Infants and
Young Children
D. Sue Schafer and Martha S. Moersch, Editors

Assessment and Application
by Sally J. Rogers and Diane B. D'Eugenio

The University of Michigan Press
Ann Arbor

Verso of Title Page

Second printing 1977
Copyright © by The University of Michigan 1977
Copyright is claimed until January, 1987. Thereafter all portions of this
work covered by this copyright will be in the public domain.
The Project presented or reported herein was performed pursuant to a grant from the
U.S. Office of Education, Department of Health, Education, and Welfare. However,
the opinions and other content do not necessarily reflect the position or policy of the
Agency, and no official endorsement should be inferred. A "First Chance" Project,
U.S. Office of Education, Bureau of Education for the Handicapped, Washington, D.C.,
G007400463.

All rights reserved. No part of this book may be reproduced or duplicated
in any form or by any means without written permission from the publisher.

ISBN 0-472-08771-1
Library of Congress Catalog Card No. 76-49257
Published in the United States of America by
The University of Michigan Press and simultaneously
in Rexdale, Canada, by John Wiley & Sons Canada, Limited
Manufactured in the United States of America

Early Intervention Project for Handicapped Infants and Young Children,
Institute for the Study of Mental Retardation and Related Disabilities,
The University of Michigan.

Half-title Page

Developmental Programming for Infants and Young Children

Volume 1

72

Title Page

Pali Text Society
TRANSLATION SERIES, No. 12

DESIGNATION OF HUMAN TYPES
(PUGGALA-PAÑÑATTI)

TRANSLATED INTO ENGLISH FOR THE
FIRST TIME BY

BIMALA CHARAN LAW, M.A., B.L.

AUTHOR OF "KSATRIYA CLANS IN BUDDHIST INDIA"; "THE LIFE
AND WORK OF BUDDHAGHOSA"; "THE BUDDHIST
CONCEPTION OF SPIRITS"; "HISTORICAL
GLEANINGS," ETC., ETC.

London
PUBLISHED FOR THE PALI TEXT SOCIETY
BY
MESSRS. LUZAC & COMPANY, LTD.
46 GREAT RUSSELL STREET, W.C.1
1969

Verso of Title Page

First published · 1924
Reprinted · · 1969

© *Pali Text Society*

EXAMPLE M15   Left Side   Double Title Page   Right Side

Anglistica & Americana

A Series of Reprints Selected by
Bernhard Fabian, Edgar Mertner,
Karl Schneider and Marvin Spevack

62

1969
GEORG OLMS VERLAG
HILDESHEIM · NEW YORK

ISAAC DISRAELI

The Works

Curiosities of Literature
Edited by Benjamin Disraeli,
Earl of Beaconsfield
(1881)

Vol. III

1969
GEORG OLMS VERLAG
HILDESHEIM · NEW YORK

Verso of Title Page   Original Title Page

Note
The present facsimile is reproduced from a copy
in the possession of the University of Münster (Eng-
lisches Seminar). Shelfmark: X1X 4020/3.
M. S.

This reprint is slightly reduced in size.

Reprografischer Nachdruck der Ausgabe London 1881
Printed in Germany
Herstellung: fotokop wilhelm weihert, Darmstadt
Best Nr. 5102 727

CURIOSITIES OF LITERATURE.

BY

ISAAC DISRAELI.

A New Edition,

EDITED, WITH MEMOIR AND NOTES.

BY HIS SON,

THE EARL OF BEACONSFIELD.

IN THREE VOLUMES.
VOL. III.

LONDON:
FREDERICK WARNE AND CO.,
BEDFORD STREET, STRAND.

74

EXAMPLE M16

Original Title Page

Reprint Title Page

THE WHORES RHETORICK
(1683)

A FACSIMILE REPRODUCTION
WITH AN INTRODUCTION BY
JAMES R. IRVINE AND G. JACK GRAVLEE

SCHOLARS' FACSIMILES AND REPRINTS
DELMAR, NEW YORK 1979

THE
Whores Rhetorick,
Calculated to the Meridian
OF
LONDON;
And conformed to the
Rules of Art.

In two Dialogues.

Id vero est, quod ego mihi puto palmarium,
Me reperisse, quomodo adolofcentulus
Meretricum ingenia, & mores posset noscere :
Mature ut cum cognorit, perpetuo oderit.

Nosse omnia hæc, falus est adolocentulis.
Terent. Eunuchus.

LONDON,
Printed for *George Shell* in *Stone-Cutter-*
Street in *Shoe-Laine.* 1683.

SCHOLARS' FACSIMILES AND REPRINTS
SERIES ESTABLISHED 1936
VOLUME 338

Published by
Scholars' Facsimiles & Reprints, Inc.
Delmar, New York 12054

Reproduced by permission of the British Library
First Printing 1979

New matter in this edition
©1979 Scholars' Facsimiles & Reprints, Inc.
All rights reserved

Printed in the United States of America

Library of Congress Cataloging in Publication Data
Main entry under title:

The Whores rhetorick (1683)

Reprint of the 1683 ed. printed for G. Shell, London.
Sometimes attributed to F. Pallavicino.
1. Pallavicino, Ferrante, 1615-1644.
PR3291.A1W5 1979   822'.4   79-17643
ISBN 0-8201-1338-7

Verso of Reprint Title Page

Title Page of Collection

AFTER

THE TEMPEST:

The Tempest, or The Enchanted Island (1670); *The*
Tempest, or The Enchanted Island (1674);
The Mock-Tempest: or The Enchanted
Castle (1675); *The Tempest.*
An Opera (1756).

INTRODUCTION BY
George Robert Guffey

WILLIAM ANDREWS CLARK
MEMORIAL LIBRARY
UNIVERSITY OF CALIFORNIA, LOS ANGELES
1969

EXAMPLE M18

Title Page

STABILITY, SECURITY, AND CONTINUITY

Mr. Justice Burton and Decision-Making in the Supreme Court 1945-1958

MARY FRANCES BERRY

Contributions in Legal Studies, Number 1

GREENWOOD PRESS
WESTPORT, CONNECTICUT • LONDON, ENGLAND

Verso of Title Page

Library of Congress Cataloging in Publication Data

Berry, Mary Frances.
    Stability, security, and continuity.

    (Contributions in legal studies; no. 1 ISSN 0147-1074)
    Bibliography: p.
    Includes index.
    1. United States. Supreme Court—History—20th century. 2. Burton, Harold Hitz, 1888-1964. 3. Judicial process—United States. I. Title. II. Series: Contributions in legal studies; no. 1.
KF8742.B47   347'.73'2634 [B]   77-84772
ISBN 0-8371-9798-8

Library of Congress Catalog Card Number: 77-84772
ISBN: 0-8371-9798-8
ISSN: 0147-1074

First published in 1978

Greenwood Press, Inc.
51 Riverside Avenue, Westport, Connecticut 06880

Printed in the United States of America

10 9 8 7 6 5 4 3 2 1

Cover & Title Page

Imprint Data on Page 2

Back & Cover + Title Page of a "With"

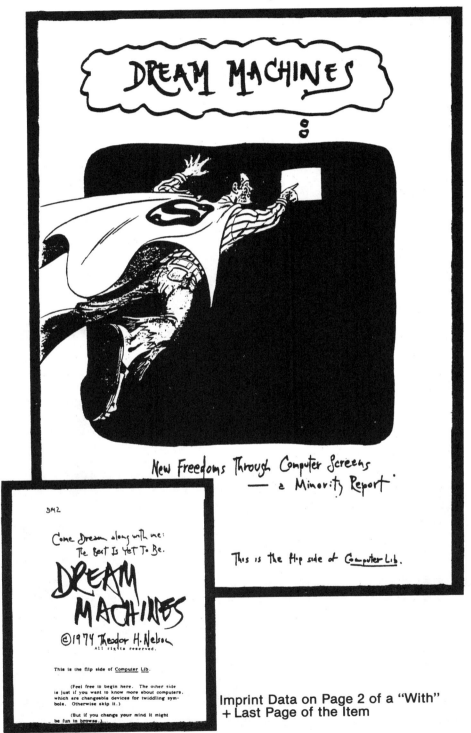

Imprint Data on Page 2 of a "With"
+ Last Page of the Item

Guide's Title Page

Centre for Educational Research and Innovation (CERI)

PIAGETIAN
INVENTORIES

**The Experiments of
JEAN PIAGET**

Verso of Guide's Title Page

© OECD, 1977
Queries concerning permissions or translation rights should be
addressed to:
Director of Information, OECD
2, rue André-Pascal, 75775 PARIS CEDEX 16, France.

ORGANISATION FOR ECONOMIC CO-OPERATION AND DEVELOPMENT
1977

Front of Container

centre
for
educational
research
and
innovation

PIAGETIAN
INVENTORIES

**The Experiments of
JEAN PIAGET**

OECD
ORGANISATION FOR ECONOMIC CO-OPERATION AND DEVELOPMENT

EXAMPLE M21

Title Page

JEAN FURSTENBERG

Le Grand Siècle
en France
et ses Bibliophiles

Volumes à Provenance,
Manuscrits et Documents de la
Fondation Furstenberg-Beaumesnil et de la
Collection Jean et Eugénie Furstenberg

Verso of Title Page

Eine deutschsprachige Kurzfassung der Einleitung findet der Leser auf Seite 145.
An English short version of the introduction is to be found on page 151.
© Copyright by Dr. Ernst Hauswedell & Co., Hamburg.
Droits de reproduction et de traduction réservés pour tous les pays, y compris l'UdSSR.
ISBN 3 7762 0027 8

Dr. Ernst Hauswedell & Co. Verlag
Hamburg 1972

Jean Furstenberg / Le Grand Siècle en France et ses Bibliophiles
Volumes à Provenance, Manuscrits et Documents
de la Fondation Furstenberg – Beaumesnil et de la Collection
Jean et Eugénie Furstenberg.

Avec 60 diapositives. Présentation générale par Richard von Sichowsky. Typographie en Monotype-Garamond et Impression par l'Imprimerie Passavia AG, Passau. Reproduction des diapositives par Herman & Kraemer OHG, Garmisch-Partenkirchen. Travaux de reliure par Verlagsbuchbinderei Ladstetter, Hamburg. Tiré à 600 exemplaires.

Mit 60 Farbdiapositiven. Die Gesamtgestaltung besorgte Richard von Sichowsky. Satz in der Monotype-Garamond und Druck durch die Druckerei Passavia AG, Passau. Die Duplikate der Diapositive lieferte die Hermann & Kraemer OHG, Garmisch-Partenkirchen. Die Einbandarbeit führte die Verlagsbuchbinderei Ladstetter, Hamburg, aus. Die Auflagenhöhe beträgt 600 Exemplare.

Colophon

Dr. Ernst Hauswedell & Co. Verlag, Hamburg 1972

EXAMPLE M22

Half-title Page

POETS ON RECORD 2
ROSEMARY DOBSON

Poets on Record General Editor: Thomas W. Shapcott

ROSEMARY DOBSON
reads from her own work

University of Queensland Press

Title Page

Published by University of Queensland Press.
St. Lucia, Queensland, 1970
The poems and notes © Rosemary Dobson.
1944, 1948, 1955, 1965, 1970
This selection and the recording © University
of Queensland Press, 1970
Typed in Press Roman 11/12 on an IBM Composer
by the University of Queensland Vari-typing Section
Printed by the University of Queensland Printery
Bound by Trade Binding Service, Pty. Ltd., Brisbane

National Library of Australia card number and
ISBN 0 7022 0682 2

Distributed by International Scholarly Book Services,
Inc. Great Britain - Europe - North America

Designed by Cyrelle

Both book and recording are copyright. Apart from
any fair dealing for the purposes of private study,
research, criticism or review, as permitted under the
Copyright Act, no part may be reproduced by any
process without written permission. Enquiries
relating to this selection, to use of the recording, and
in broadcast rights, should be made to the publishers.

NOTE

The accompanying record should be played at
45 r.p.m.

Verso of Title Page

82

EXAMPLE M23

Title Page

Hypnotic Realities

The Induction of Clinical Hypnosis and Forms of Indirect Suggestion

by

Milton H. Erickson

Ernest L. Rossi

Sheila I. Rossi

With a Foreword by André M. Weitzenhoffer

IRVINGTON PUBLISHERS, Inc., New York

Halsted Press Division of

JOHN WILEY & Sons

New York   London   Toronto   Sydney

Verso of Title Page

Distributed by HALSTED PRESS.
A Division of JOHN WILEY & SONS, New York

Library of Congress in Publication Data
Erickson, Milton H.
    Hypnotic Realities

    Bibliography: p.
    1. Hypnotism—Therapeutic use. I. Rossi, Ernest Lawrence, joint author. II. Rossi, Sheila I., joint author III. Title
RC495.E72   615'.8512   76-20636
ISBN 0-470-15169-2

Printed in The United States of America

Example M1 (Monograph): Statement of Responsibility in Title Proper

Burney, Frances, 1752-1840.
    The journals and letters of Fanny Burney (Madame
d'Arblay) [text] / edited by Joyce Hemlow ; with
Curtis D. Cecil . . . [et al.]. -- Oxford : Clarendon
Press, 1972-
    v. : ill., facsims., geneal. tables, ports. ;
23 cm.
    Includes index.
    ISBN 0-19-812467-8 (v. 5). -- ISBN 0-19-812526-X
(corrected) (v. 6)

    I. Hemlow, Joyce, ed. II. Title.

Pre-AACR 2

Arblay, Frances (Burney) d', 1752-1840.
    The journals and letters of Fanny Burney (Madame
D'Arblay). Oxford, Clarendon Press, 1972-
    v. illus., facsim., geneal. table, port. 23 cm.
    Vol. 2 edited by Joyce Hemlow and Althea Douglas.
    Contents: v. 1. 1791-1792, letters 1-39.--v. 2.
Courtship and marriage 1793, letters 40-121.--v. 3.
Great Bookham 1793-1797, letters 122-240.--v. 4. West
Humble 1797-1801, letters 251-422.

(LC copy; source of cataloging is Great Britain)

Discussion

Description:

Title and statement of responsibility area. Since the name of the author of the journals and letters is part of the title, her name is not repeated in the statement of responsibility (Rules 1.1F13 and 1.1B2). Rather than giving the editor's name in a note, as in the pre-AACR 2 record, it is transcribed as a subsequent statement of responsibility. Hemlow is the editor of all the volumes published to date; only the secondary editors vary; therefore only the name of the first secondary editor of the initial volume was transcribed. Ellipses and [et al.] are given to indicate the omission of the other names (Rule 1.1F5).

Note area. The addition of a formal contents note is an option (Rule 0.27) which we chose not to take since the set will be complete in 10 volumes. This, and the extended period of time it will take to complete the set, lead to the decision to omit the formal contents note given in the pre-AACR 2 record.

Access points:

Main entry. In both records the author of the correspondence is the main entry; only the form of the name differs. The AACR 2 record displays the form of name formulated according to the new rules (Rules 22.2A-B); references should tie the old form to the new; this will be of particular importance since the new form was previously the "see" reference.

Added entries. Added access was also provided for the main editor (Rule 21.30D) of the six volumes published thus far. A title added entry is given applying Rule 21.30J.

Example M2 (Monograph): Adaptation

> Marowitz, Charles
> A Macbeth [text] : freely adapted from Shakespeare's tragedy / Charles Marowitz. -- London : Calder and Boyars, 1971.
> 106 p., [6] p. of plates : ill. ; 21 cm. -- (Playscript ; 45)
> ISBN 0-7145-0719-9 (cloth ed.). -- ISBN 0-7145-0720-2 (paper ed.)
>
> I. Shakespeare, William, 1564-1616. Macbeth.
> II. Title.

Pre-AACR 2

> Marowitz, Charles.
> A Macbeth: freely adapted from Shakespeare's tragedy. London, Calder and Boyars, 1971.
> 106 p. illus. 21 cm. (Playscript, 45)
>
> I. Shakespeare, William, 1564-1616. Macbeth.
> II. Title.

(LC copy)

Discussion

Description:

General statement. The general descriptive part of each record is identical, with the exception of the prescribed punctuation and its required spacing.

Physical description area. The collation of this record has the first substantive change in the addition of the number of plates contained in the item (Rule 2.5B10). This change had already appeared in AACR Chapter 6, revised (1974).

Note area. The addition of ISBD has also been in use since Chapter 6, revised. The ISBN (Rule 1.8B) was not required in AACR 1 since, quite simply, it did not exist at the time the rules were published. Its precursor, the standard book number, began to appear in 1968.

Access points:

Main entry. The main entry is identical for both records; the rule for adaptations has not changed (AACR 1 Rule 7; AACR 2 Rule 21.10); it is, however, more clearly and succinctly stated.

Added entries. The added entry under the author and title of the original work is in accordance with the same rules. A title added entry is also made (Rule 21.30J).

Example M3 (Monograph): Later Edition with Secondary Edition Statement

> Gray, Henry, 1825-1861.
>   Anatomy [text] : descriptive and surgical / by Henry Gray ; with five hundred and twenty-two engravings on wood, the drawings by H.V. Carter and Dr. Westmacott, the dissections jointly by the author and Dr. Carter ; with an introduction on general anatomy and development by T. Holmes. -- A new American [ed.], from the 8th and enl. English ed. / to which was added Landmarks : medical and surgical by Luther Holden. -- Philadelphia : H.C. Lea, 1878.
>   xxx, 983 [i.e. 951] p. : ill. ; 27 cm.
>
> I. Homer, Timothy, 1825-1907. II. Holden, Luther, 1815-1905. III. Title.

Pre-AACR 2

> Gray, Henry, 1825-1861.
>   Anatomy, descriptive and surgical. By Henry Gray. With five hundred and twenty-two engravings on wood. The drawings by H.V. Carter and Dr. Westmacott. The dissections jointly by the author and Dr. Carter. With an introduction on general anatomy and development by T. Holmes. A new American [ed.] from the 8th and enl. English ed., to which is added Landmarks, medical and surgical, by Luther Holden. Philadelphia, Henry C. Lea, 1878.
>   xxx, 33-983 p. illus. 27 cm.
>
> I. Holmes, Timothy, 1825-1905. II. Holden, Luther, 1815-1905. III. Title.

(not LC copy)

Discussion

Description:

Title and statement of responsibility area. The use of the title "Dr." in the statement of responsibility is permissible according to Rule 1.1F7b, if omission would leave only the surname. This rule was also applicable in AACR 1 Chapter 6, revised, but not stated explicitly in the original Chapter 6. All secondary statements were transcribed according to Rule 1.1F6. The order is that of the title page and was not changed, which is permissible under the same rule. All the information on the illustrations was treated as one statement and the different parts were separated by commas. The rules do not specify what to do in such a case; therefore, it seemed to be a reasonable solution not to treat them as individual statements of responsibility.

Edition area. The abbreviation "ed." was interpolated for grammatical reasons. The second edition statement was separated from the first by a comma (,) (Rule 1.2E1). AACR 1 makes no reference to secondary edition statements nor to the statements of responsibility relating to the edition. Chapter 6, revised, because of the ISBD influence, adds the statement of responsibility relating to the edition, although in practice librarians have transcribed this information in the same order.

Physical description area. More than one rule was consulted for the collation. Rule 2.5B5, AACR 2, recommends giving only the last numbered page when the numbering changes from roman to arabic without changing the actual number of pages contained in a volume. However, this information would not be correct for this title since there is a three-page gap between the roman numeral "xxx" and the first arabic numeral "33." AACR 1 Rule 142, 3rd sentence (Chapter 6, revised Rule 141B1e) is identical to 2.5B5 in AACR 2. In the same section in Chapter 6, revised, the AACR 2 Rule 2.5B4 is treated, and by applying this rule we arrive at the pagination as it appears in the above record.

Access points:

Main entry. The main entry under either rule is the same (Rule 21.A1).

Added entries. Added entries were provided for the author of the introduction, since it appeared to be of importance to this edition, and for the author of "Landmarks," which had been added to this edition. Rule 21.30C was followed in both instances since Holmes is prominently named on the title page, and "Landmarks" is also given a prominent position on the title page.

Example M4 (Monograph): Later Edition Entered Under Reviser

> Burnside, John W.
>   Adams' physical diagnosis [text] : an introduction
> to clinical medicine / John W. Burnside. --
> 15th ed. -- Baltimore : Williams & Wilkins,
> 1975, c1974.
>   xi, 223 p. : ill. ; 26 cm.
>   Previous eds.: R.C. Cabot. 1st-11th ed. (1st-
> 2nd ed. titled: Physical diagnosis of diseases of
> the chest)--R.C. Cabot, F.D. Adams. 12th-13th
> ed.--F.D. Adams. 14th ed.
>   Includes index.

(cont'd.)

I. Cabot, Richard C. (Richard Clarke), 1868-1936.
II. Adams, F. Dennette (Frank Dennette), 1892-
Physical diagnosis. III. Title. IV. Title:
Physical diagnosis.

Pre-AACR 2

Adams, Frank Dennette, 1892-
Adams' Physical diagnosis; an introduction to
clinical medicine. 15th ed. [by] John W. Burnside.
Baltimore, Williams & Wilkins [1974]
xi, 223 p. illus. 26 cm.
First-11th ed. by R.C. Cabot (1st-2d ed., with
title: Physical diagnosis of diseases of the chest);
12th-13th ed. by R.C. Cabot and F.D. Adams;
14th ed. by F.D. Adams.

I. Burnside, John W., ed. II. Cabot, Richard
Clarke, 1868-1939. Physical diagnosis of the
chest. III. Title; IV. Title; Physical diagnosis.

(LC copy; correction made to last phrase in note.)

Discussion

Description:

Title and statement of responsibility area. The transcription of the bibliographic data
follows the normal pattern. "Adams," the name of one of the authors of the previous editions, remains part of the title, and Burnside's name appears as the statement of responsibility element. An author's name is not transposed to its customary position when it forms an
integral grammatical part of the title proper (Rules 1.1B2 and 1.1F3).

Edition area. In this area the records differ widely. We decided to record Burnside's
name in the first area as the editor of the 15th edition. Consequently, this area contains only
the ordinal number of the edition. (The rationale for this decision is given under main entry
below.)

Note area. We decided to change the form of the note and follow the instructions of
Rule 1.7A3, "Form of notes. Order of information." Thus in the example the author of the
previous edition(s) is given before the edition statement. The variation of the title of the first
two editions is given in the same manner as in the previous record.

Access points:

Main entry. Burnside was chosen as the main entry in accordance with Rule 21.12B.
The chief source of information (the title page) appears to give Burnside the responsibility

for the work. The text itself, consisting of only 223 pages, is a great deal briefer than the 14th ed. The introduction also states: "This is less the fifteenth edition of a textbook than it is the fifteenth edition of a concept." AACR 1 choice of entry was derived from Rule 14.A, "Reviser vs. original author."

Added entries. Added access was given to the authors and titles of the earlier editions to make a library user aware of the later work, as is suggested by Rule 21.12B. Title access was also provided (Rule 21.30J). The second title (IV. Title:) should be made only if the library does not have a dictionary catalog or if it has an online catalog with a separate subject file.

Example M5 (Monograph): Conference/Meeting with Parallel Title & Complex Statement of Responsibility

> Die Entstehung der Schizophrenie [text] = The origin of
>   schizophrenia / hrsg. von M. Bleuler und J. Angst ;
>   unter Mitarbeit von J. Angst ... [et al.]. --
> Bern : H. Huber, c1971.
> 119 p. : ill. ; 23 cm. -- (Aktuelle Probleme in der
> Psychiatrie, Neurologie, Neurochirugie ; Bd. 5)
>   "Symposium zum 100jährignen Bestehen der Psychia-
> trischen Universitätsklinik Burghölzli-Zürich und zu
> Ehren von Professor Dr. Manfred Bleuler (am 3./4.
> Juli 1970 in Zürich)." -- t.p. verso,
>   English or German.
>   Includes bibliographies.
>
>   I. Bleuler, M. (Manfred), ed. II. Angst, J. (Jules),
> ed. III. Universität Zürich. Psychiatrische Klinik.
> IV. Title: The origin of schizophrenia.

> **Pre-AACR 2**
>
> Die Entstehung der Schizophrenie. The origin of
>   schizophrenia. (Symposium zum 100jährigen Bestehen
>   der Psychiatrischen Universitätsklinik Burghölzli-
>   Zürich am.3./4. Juli 1970 in Zürich). Hrsg. von
>   M(anfred) Bleuler und J(ules) Angst. Unter Mitarb.
>   von J. Angst u.a. . Bern, Stuttgart, Wien, Hans
>   Huber, (1971).
> 119 p. 23 cm. (Aktuelle Probleme in der Psychiatrie,
> Neurologie, Neurochirurgie, Bd. 5)
>   English or German.
>   Includes bibliographies.
>
>   I. Bleuler, Manfred, ed. II. Angst, Jules, ed. III.
> Zürich. Universität. Psychiatrische Klinik. IV.
> Title: The origin of schizophrenia.

(LC copy ; apparently part of the overseas cataloging agreements, since most of the transcription after the parallel title does not even conform to AACR 1 or any other previous rules.)

Discussion

Description:

Title and statement of responsibility area. The title page displays a parallel title and parallel statement of responsibility; the latter is not recorded as such since the English statement is mixed with German by the conjunction "und" (Rule 1.1F11, paragraph 2). The handling of the names in the author statement/statement of responsibility area in the AACR 1 record, as well as the transcription, are neither AACR 1 nor Chapter 6, revised. An examination of the record in the National Union Catalog gives Switzerland as the source of cataloging. The universal application of ISBDs will bring descriptive cataloging to greater conformity and so ease exchange of bibliographic data.

In AACR 1 the rules on parallel titles are quite complex, and generally would permit only the recording of one parallel title, but never a parallel statement of responsibility/authorship.

The prescribed punctuation makes the real difference in the transcription of the title page since Rule 1.11F11 was not applied. Had it been applied, a parallel statement of responsibility would have also been given in the area and the record would appear as follows:

> Die Enstehung der Schizophrenie / Hrsg. von M. Bleuler und
> J. Angst = The origin of schizophrenia / edited by M.
> Bleuler ... J. Angst ; unter Mitarbeit von J. Angst
> ... [et al.]. ....

Note area. The note linking the title to the symposium was transcribed in this area. It does not appear in the chief source of information but was judged useful information and given a quoted note; its source is also given (Rule 1.7A3).

Access points:

Main entry. The title main entry was chosen according to 21.1C 3, since neither Rules 21.1A nor 21.B (personal or corporate responsibility for the work) applies.

Added entries. Added access was provided for both editors according to Rule 21.30D which suggests an added entry "...for a prominently named editor or compiler of a monographic work." An additional access point under the name of the clinic appeared useful since its centennary existence was celebrated at the unnamed symposium. Rule 21.30H permits added entries of this nature.

Example M6 (Monograph): Conference/Meeting with Conference Name in Note Area

> The industrial composition of income and product [text] / John W.
>   Kendrick, editor. -- New York : National Bureau of
>   Economic Research ; Distributed by Columbia University
>   Press, 1968.
>   viii, 494 p. : ill. ; 24 cm. -- (Studies in income and
> wealth ; v. 32)
>   "Conference on the Industrial Composition of Income and
> Product held on December 12, 1966, at the Brookings Institution
> in Washington, D.C."--Prefatory note.
>   Includes bibliographic references.
>
> I. Kendrick, John W., ed. II. Conference on the Industrial
> Composition of Income and Product (1969 : Brookings Institu-
> tion) III. National Bureau of Economic Research. IV.
> Brookings Institution.

Pre-AACR 2

> Conference on the Industrial Composition of Income and
>   Product, Brookings Institution, 1969.
>   The industrial composition of income and product;
> [papers] John W. Kendrick, editor. New York,
> National Bureau of Economic Research; distributed by
> Columbia University Press, 1968.
>   viii, 494 p. illus. 24 cm. (Studies in income and
> wealth, v. 32)
>   Includes bibliographical references.
>
> I. Kendrick, John W., ed. II. National Bureau of
> Economic Research. III. Brookings Institution,
> Washington, D.C. IV. Title.

(not LC copy)

Discussion

Description:

Title and statement of responsibility. AACR 1 (Rule 133E 1) and AACR 2 (Rule 1.1E6) both allow additions to the title "If the title proper needs explanation..." This need can be obvious at times and at others it can be a matter of personal judgment. In the AACR 2 example, we decided not to follow the LC pattern to add the qualifier "papers." Since the title proper is distinct and the conference is no longer the main entry its name is given only in the note area. Otherwise the two records are very similar up through the dimensions of the physical description; the exception is the prescribed punctuation and its related spacing. "Distributed" is capitalized in accordance with Appendix Rule A.7B, "Initial words or abbreviations not part of the name."

Series area. The series is identical in form to Pre-AACR 2: only the punctuation and spacing differ. Although the name of the conference, which is responsible for the series title, is prominently named on the title page, we did not transcribe it in the series area. Rule 1.6E1, which deals with the statement of responsibility relating to the series, says that the statement should only be transcribed when it is necessary to identify the series title. That was not the circumstance here.

Notes area. The conference data appeared in the prefatory note and was quoted from that source. Rule 1.7A3 requires that the source of a quoted note be given when it is not the chief source of information. The note is required by Rule 21.29F in order to provide an added entry for the conference since it is not named in the body of the bibliographic description.

Access points:

Main entry. The main entry is under title rather than under the conference name. A conference is a corporate body (21.1B1) and as such Rule 21.1B2 must be applied for the selection of the body as a main entry; here 21.1B2d would apply. This rule, however, states that the conference is the main entry "...provided that the conference, expedition, or event is prominently named in the item being catalogued." It is now necessary to look at the definition of "prominently" given under 0.8, which states that the word "...means that a statement to which it applies must be a formal statement found in one of the prescribed sources of information (see 1.0A)..." The chief source of information for the statement of responsibility is the title page (Rule 2.0B2). In this example the conference is named in a prefatory note on the verso of the title page; therefore the choice for the main entry is the title (Rule 21.1C 2).

Added entries. Added access is provided for the editor who is prominently named on the title page. The conference and the institution where the conference took place are both of importance to individuals knowing about them and possibly wanting to retrieve them by these names. Therefore, they are mentioned in the note area and receive added access points. The prominence of the National Bureau of Economic Research in the field of economics and on the title page also justifies added access to this body. Rule 21.29B makes very broad provisions for added access and can easily be applied to this title.

Example M7 (Monograph): Conference/Meeting with Main Entry Under Conference Name

> International Glaucoma Symposium (1978 : Nara)
>   Glaucoma update [text] : International Glaucoma
> Symposium, Nara, Japan, May 7-11, 1978 / editors
> G.K. Krieglstein and W. Leydhecker. -- Berlin ;
> New York : Springer, 1979.
>   xiv, 224 p. : ill., ; 25 cm.
>   Includes bibliographical references and index.
>   ISBN 3-540-09350-8. -- ISBN 0-387-09350-8.
>
> I. Krieglstein, G.K., ed. II. Leydhecker, W., ed.
> III. Title.

Pre-AACR 2

International Glaucoma Symposium, Nara, Japan, 1978.
    Glaucoma update : International Glaucoma Symposium,
Nara, Japan, May 7-11, 1978 / editors G. K. Krieglstein
and W. Leydhecker. -- Berlin ; New York : Springer-
Verlag, 1979.
    xiv, 224 p. : ill. ; 25 cm.
    Includes bibliographies and index.
    ISBN 0-387-09350-8

    I. Krieglstein, G. K.   II. Leydhecker, Wolfgang.
    III. Title.

(LC copy; AACR 1, Chapter 6, revised)

Discussion

Description:

General statement. The AACR 2 record and the one cataloged according to the rules of
AACR 1, Chapter 6, revised, are nearly identical. They differ only in the spacing between
the initials; spaces are not needed in abbreviations with internal punctuation (see University
of Chicago Press: *A Manual of Style,* p. 316, item 14.2). The other difference is in the imprint;
the AACR 2 record does not contain the word "Verlag" (publisher), which was probably
transcribed through an oversight.

The difference in the note between "bibliographical references" and "bibliographies" is
a matter of interpretation and not of substance.

Access points:

Main entry. The prominence of the symposium on the title page, the chief source of information, requires entry under the conference, i.e., the corporate body (Rule 21.1B2 d).
The difference is in the AACR 2 form, which will be discussed in a later chapter.

Added entries. Added access is provided for the editor or editors if they are prominently named on the chief source of information, as in the case here (Rule 21.30D). The function
designator was added to the names; it is an option provided by AACR 2. The initials in the
first named added entry also do not have a space dividing them.

Example M8 (Monograph): Shared Responsibility / Corporate Bodies

A guide to planning and conducting environmental study area
    workshops [text] / developed cooperatively by National
    Education Association and National Park Service, U.S.
    Dept. of the Interior. -- Washington, D.C. : NEA, 1972.
    50 p. : ill. ; 27 cm.
    Selected references: p. [49]-50.
    NEA stock no. 381-11998.

(cont'd.)

I. National Education Association (U.S.). II.
National Park Service (U.S.).

Pre-AACR 2

National Education Association of the United States.
   A guide to planning and conducting environmental
study area workshops. Developed cooperatively by
National Education Association and National Park
Service, U.S. Dept. of the Interior. Washington,
D.C., NEA [1972]
   50 p. illus. 27 cm.
   Selected bibliography: p. [49]-50.

I. U.S. National Park Service. II. Title.

(not LC copy)

Discussion

Description:

General statement. The descriptions of the two records do not differ a great deal from
one another. The exceptions are the punctuation and the lack of square brackets around the
imprint date. The more precise delineation of sources of description and, at the same time,
their expansion to parts other than the title page reduces the use of brackets in the body of
the bibliographic description.

Note area. AACR 1 makes no reference to numbers on an item and Chapter 6, revised,
refers only to the ISBN. AACR 2 recognizes the importance of such numbers for item identification and acquisition (Rule 1.7B19). However, notes are optional and not all libraries
may wish to add this data to their records.

Access points:

Main entry. Although the statement of responsibility contains two corporate bodies, to
whom authorship has been attributed, the work does not really fit under any of the five
categories which permit entry under corporate body (Rule 21.1B2). The only rule which
comes close is 21.1B2 c, which permits entry under the body if the work represents its collective thought. AACR 1 would have required entry under the first named corporate body.

Added entries. Access is also provided to the names of the two bodies given in the
statement of responsibility (Rule 21.30E, "Corporate bodies"). Thus, as in AACR 1, the
item can be located under either body and the title, even though the main entry is the title.

Example M9 (Monograph): Shared Responsibility / Personal Names

> Katz, Sedelle, 1923-
>   Understanding the rape victim [text] : a synthesis
> of research findings / Sedelle Katz, Mary Ann Mazur.
> -- New York : Wiley, c1979.
>   xvii, 340 p. ; 23 cm. -- (Wiley series on
> personality processes)
>   "A Wiley Interscience Publication."
>   Bibliography: p. 317-330.
>   Includes index.
>   0-471-03573-4 : $17.95.
>
>   I. Mazur, Mary Ann, 1946- . II. Title.

Pre-AACR 2

> Katz, Sedelle, 1923-
>   Understanding the rape victim : a synthesis
> of research findings / Sedelle Katz, Mary Ann
> Mazur. -- New York : Wiley, c1979.
>   xvii, 340 p. ; 23 cm. -- (Wiley series on
> personality processes)
>   "A Wiley Interscience Publication."
>   Bibliography: p. 317-330.
>   Includes index.
>   ISBN 0-471-03573-4.
>
>   I. Mazur, Mary Ann, 1946- . II. Title.

(LC copy; AACR 1, Chapter 6, revised)

Discussion

Description:

Title and statement of responsibility area. The transcription of this title presents no problems. The two records are identical with the exception of the GMD (general material designation) which we added to the AACR 2 record. However, a minor problem with the AACR 2 rules is that they do not provide guidance for the treatment of multiple authors as the earlier rules do. Yet, the general introduction (under "Style") recommends the use of the *Chicago Style Manual* for punctuation not covered or prescribed by the rules. Consulting this or any other source dealing with punctuation, we learn that words and phrases in a series are separated by a comma (,). This is the answer to the problem.

Note area. The note was transcribed from the title page, where it appeared in a prominent place, and will not need to be qualified by its source, like other quoted notes (Rule 1.7A3). The note is not a publisher's series but could be described as the publisher's program; Wiley's Interscience Publications is a division of the corporation.

Access points:

Main entry. The main entry is for the first author named, in case of shared responsibility, when the principal responsibility cannot be determined (Rule 21.6C).

Added entries. Added entries for the other authors (not more than two) are always provided when the above-named rule applies. Title added entry should also be made in cases of entry under personal name, corporate body or uniform title (21.30J).

Example M10 (Monograph): Committee Report / Corporate Responsibility

> President's Commission on Income Maintenance Programs.
> Poverty amid plenty [text] : the American paradox / the report of the President's Commission on Income Maintenance Programs. -- Washington, D.C. : For sale by the Supt. of Doc., G.P.O., 1969.
> ix, 155 p. : ill. ; 25 cm.
> Includes bibliographical references.
>
> I. Title.

> **Pre-AACR 2**

> United States. President's Commission on Income Maintenance Programs.
> Poverty amid plenty; the American paradox; report.
> Washington, For sale by the Supt. of Docs., U.S. Govt. Print. Off. 1969.
> ix, 155 p. illus. 25 cm.
> Includes bibliographical references.
>
> I. Title.

(LC copy)

Discussion

Description:

Title and statement of responsibility area. In the description only the statement of responsibility may present a problem. The phrase "the report of the" could be interpreted either as other title information or as describing the role of the body. Rule 1.1F12 deals with this type of statement and gives an easy way out in cases of doubt, suggesting that the phrase be treated as the statement of responsibility. This rule is related to 1.1E4 which includes the statement of responsibility in the other title information when it forms an integral part.

Publication, distribution, etc. area. The U.S. Govt. Print. Off. abbreviation has become simply G.P.O., analogous to the British H.M.S.O. (each is the government's printing office).

Access points:

Main entry. The corporate main entry was selected as the main entry according to Rule 21.1B2c since the title is the "record of the collective thought of the body," a commission.

Added entries. Rule 21.30J requires an added entry under the title proper when the main entry is either a personal name or a corporate body, the latter being the case here.

Example M11 (Monograph): Committee Report / Personal Name Main Entry

> Phaff, J.M.L.
>   Midwives in Europe [text] : present and future education
> and role of the midwife in Council of Europe member
> states and in Finland : report / prepared by J.M.L.
> Phaff, L. Sassi, L. Valvanne ; presented by E.J. Hickl.
> -- Strasbourg : Council of Europe ; [New York (225 Lafayette
> St., New York, N.Y. 10012.) : Sold by Manhattan Pub. Co.], 1975.
>   68 p. : ill. ; 24 cm.
>   At head of title: European Public Health Committee.
> Co-ordinated Medical Research (1974 Programme).
>
>   I. Sassi, L. II. Valvanne, L. III. Council of Europe.
> European Public Health Committee.

Pre-AACR2

> Phaff, J. M. L.
>   Midwives in Europe : present and future education
> and role of the midwife in Council of Europe member
> states and in Finland : report / prepared by J. M.
> L. Phaff, L. Sassi, L. Valvanne ; presented by E.
> J. Hickl. -- Strasbourg : Council of Europe ; [New
> York : sold by Manhattan Pub. Co.], 1975.
>   68 p. : ill. ; 24 cm.
>   At head of title: European Public Health Committee.
> Co-ordinated Medical Research (1974 Programme).
>
>   I. Sassi, L., joint author. II. Valvanne, L.,
> joint author. III. Council of Europe.
> European Public Health Committee.

(LC copy; AACR 1 Chapter 6, revised. Copy contained "Fellowship," after "Research," in the note; it was assumed that this was a transcription error and has not been transcribed.)

Discussion

Description:

General statement. Both records are very similar up to the imprint or publication, distribution, etc. area. The Pre-AACR 2 record was cataloged according to Chapter 6, revised, and thus does not differ even in the punctuation or spacing.

The transcription of initials without interceding spaces is a minor variation between the two records. In actuality the LC record should not display spaces between the initials either and the G.P.O. *Style Manual* has been followed. The *Chicago Style Manual* also does not recommend spacing in abbreviations with internal periods (see p. 316, item 14.2).

Publication, distribution, etc. area. The addition to this area is the address of the U.S. distributor of the publication. This information is readily available from the last page. The optional addition, Rule 1.4C7, permits the transcription of this type of data for publishers not considered major.

Access points:

Main entry. The choice for main entry is the first author named, if more than one appear on the title page and the principal responsibility is not indicated (Rule 21.6C).

Added entries. Access is also provided for the names of the two joint authors (Rule 21.30B) and the committee according to 21.30E, since its name is given prominently on the title page, the chief source of information.

Example M12 (Monograph): Multipart Item (Set) : Complex Editors' Statement

A manual of the writings in Middle English, 1050-
    1500 [text] / by members of the Middle English Group of the
Modern Language Association of America ; J. Burke Severs,
general editor ; Albert E. Hartung, general editor. -- New
Haven ; Connecticut Academy of Arts and Sciences ;
Hamden, Conn. (995 Sherman Ave., Hamden, Conn. 06514) : Archon
Books, 1967-
    v. ; 24 cm.
Vols. 1-2, edited by J. Burke Severs; vols. 3- ,
edited by Albert E. Hartung.
    "Based upon A manual of the writings in Middle
English 1050-1400 / by John Edwin Wells. New Haven,
1916, and Supplements 1-9, 1919-1951."
    ISBN 0-208-01342-3 (v. 2). -- ISBN 0-208-01220-6
(v. 3). -- ISBN 0-208-01342-3 (v. 4). -- ISBN
0-208-01459-4 (v. 5).

I. Severs, J. Burke (John Burke), ed. II. Hartung,
Albert E., 1923-   , ed. III. Modern Language Assoc-
iation of America. Middle English Group. IV. Wells,
John Edwin, 1875-1943. A manual of the writings in
Middle English, 1050-1400.

Example M15 (Monograph): Reprint/Multipart Item (Set)

>
> Disraeli, Isaac, 1776-1848.
>   Curiosities of literature [text] / Isaac Disraeli ;
> edited by Benjamin Disraeli, Earl of Beacons-
> field. -- Hildesheim ; New York : G. Olms, 1969.
>   3 v. : ill., ports., facsim. ; 18 cm. -- (The
> works / Isaac Disraeli ; v. 3) (Anglistica & Americana ;
> 62)
>   Originally published: London : Frederick
> Warne, 1881.
>   Facsimile of Mr. Pope's Manuscript Homer
> inserted at end of v. 3.
>   "This reprint is slightly reduced in size." --
> T.p. of verso.
>   Includes index.
>
>   I. Disraeli, Benjamin, Earl of Beaconsfield, 1808-1881., ed. II.
> Title.

Pre-AACR 2

>
> Disraeli, Isaac, 1776-1848.
>   Curiosities of literature. Edited by Benjamin
> Disraeli, Earl of Beaconsfield. Hildesheim, George Olms, 1969.
>   3 v. illus. ports. facsim. 18 cm. (His The
> works, v. 3) (Anglistica & Americana, 62)
>   Reprint of the 1881 ed., published by Frederick
> Warne, London.
>   "This reprint is slightly reduced in size."
>   Facsimile of Mr. Pope's Manuscript Homer inserted
> at end of v. 3.
>   Includes index.

I. Beaconsfield, Benjamin Disraeli, 1st Earl of,
1808-1881, ed. II. Title.

(not LC copy)

Discussion

Description:

Title and statement of responsibility area. The author and the editor are both recorded since they appear in prominent positions on the title page. The difference between AACR 1 and AACR 2 is that the author does not have to be recorded according to AACR 1 if the form of the name for a personal author is identical to that in the main entry heading. (AACR 2 Rule 1.0D1, first level of description, likewise does not require this.)

Publication, distribution, etc. area. Both AACR 2 and AACR 1, Chapter 6, revised, re-quire a second place of publication if that place is located in the country of the cataloging agency. AACR 1, as the record shows, required only the first named place, particularly if that is the actual place of publication.

Series area. An author series is no longer treated as "His," "Hers," "Their" or "Its" but the "title / author sequence" is followed as in the first area: the title and statement of responsibility area of transcription. The statement of responsibility is required by AACR 2 only if it identifies the series, clearly the case here (Rule 1.6E1).

Note area. Rule 1.7A3 requires that the order of the notes follow the areas of description to which they relate. The "Edition and history" note is a formal note (Rule 1.7A3, "Formal notes") and is preceded by an "invariable phrase," followed by a colon (:). Prescribed punctuation is applied to the note data. The corresponding note in the pre-AACR 2 record is free form. The quoted note relating to size is followed in the AACR 2 record by an indication of its source (Rule 1.7A3, "Quotations").

Access points:

Main entry. With a single author no choice is necessary and the rules do not differ here.

Added entries. An added entry was provided according to Rule 21.30D, because the editor's name appears prominently on the title page and also because of his own importance.

Example M16 (Monograph): Reprint / Anonymous Work

> The whores rhetorick (1683) [text] : a facsimile reproduction
>   / with an introduction by James R. Irvine and G. Jack Gravlee.
>   -- Delmar, N.Y. : Scholars' Facsimiles and Reprints, 1979.
>   xii, 222 p. ; 23 cm. -- (Scholars' facsimiles and reprints ; v. 338)
>   Sometimes attributed to Ferrante Pallavicino.
>   Also attributed to Sir Roger L'Estrange. Cf. S. Haskell,
> Dict. of anonymous and pseudonymous English literature.
>   Originally published: London : printed for G. Shell, 1683.
>
>   I. Pallavicino, Ferrante, 1615-1644. II. L'Estrange, Sir
> Roger, 1616-1704.

Pre-AACR 2

> The whores rhetorick (1683) : a facsimile reproduction /
> with an introduction by James R. Irvine and G. Jack
> Gravlee. -- Delmar, N.Y. : Scholars' Facsimiles and Reprints,
> 1979.
>   264 p. in various pagings : facsim. ; 23 cm. -- (Scholars'
> facsimiles and reprints ; v. 338)
>   Reprint of the 1683 ed., printed for G. Shell, London.
>   Sometimes attributed to Ferrante Pallavicino.
>
>   I. Pallavicino, Ferrante, 1615-1644.

(LC copy; AACR 1, Chapter 6, revised. The series statement was added, however.)

Discussion

Description:

General statement. In toto, the pre-AACR 2 description corresponds closely to AACR 2. The major exception is the physical description area.

Physical description area. The new rules require that all sequences of page numberings be given (2.5B2) and that unnumbered sections not be recorded (2.5B3) unless the sequences constitute the whole or make up a substantial part; this is not the case here. The difference in the illustration information is a matter of personal interpretation. We decided not to consider the copy of the original title page as a facsimile, which may have been done for the pre-AACR 2 record since the original title page is the only illustrative matter.

Note area. The order of notes was reversed, since AACR 2 requires that the notes appear in the sequence of the area of description to which they belong. The statement of responsibility element comes before the edition area. A second statement of responsibility note was added and its source quoted, since the information comes from outside. No source is required for data in a note if the information comes from within the item.

Access points:

Main entry. The main entry is under title according to Rule 21.1C, first alternative; the personal authorship is not known with certainty.

Added entries. These were provided for both possible authors (Rule 21.29B). The statement of responsibility "with an introduction . . ." is a secondary statement and would have been preceded by the statement of responsibility for the item had there been one. No added access was provided for these two individuals; their contribution to the work as a whole is not significant. None of the rules under 21.30 seem to apply.

Note the position of "Sir" in the second added entry. The name was formulated according to Rule 22.12B, "British title of honour." The Library of Congress will continue to have the title of nobility in all cases follow the given name (e.g., L'Estrange, Roger, Sir, 1616-1704). The justification for this decision is that machine filing at this time cannot handle the "Sir" in this position.

Example M17 (Monograph): Reprint / Collective Title

> After The tempest [text] / introduction by George Robert
>   Guffey. -- Los Angeles : William Andrews Clark Memorial
>   Library, University of California, 1969.
>   290 p. in various pagings ; 22 cm.
>   Reprints of the originals of four 17th through 18th
> century adaptations of Shakespeare's The tempest.
>   Contents: The tempest, or The enchanted island
> (1670) -- The tempest, or The enchanted island (1674)
> -- The mock-tempest, or The enchanted castle (1675). /
> T. Duffet. -- The tempest : an opera (1756).
>   Includes bibliographical references.   (cont'd.)

I. Shakespeare, William, 1564-1616. The tempest (1969). II. Duffet, T. (Thomas). The mock-tempest (1969). III. Smith, John Christopher, 1712-1795. The tempest. Libretto (1969). IV. Guffey, George Robert.

Pre-AACR 2

After The tempest: The tempest; or, The enchanted island (1670); The tempest; or, The enchanted island (1674); The mock-tempest; or The enchanted castle (1675); The tempest; an opera (1756). Introd. by George Robert Guffey. Los Angeles, William Andrews Clark Memorial Library, University of California, 1969.
1 v. (various pagings) 23 cm.
Includes bibliographical references.

I. Shakespeare, William, 1564-1616. The tempest. 1969. II. Duffet, Thomas, fl. 1678. The mock-tempest. 1969. III. Smith, John Christopher, 1712-1795. The tempest. Libretto. English. 1969. IV. Guffey, George Robert, ed. V. California. University at Los Angeles. William Andrews Clark Memorial Library.

(LC copy)

Discussion

Description:

Title and statement of responsibility area. According to Rule 21.1B2, only the title proper is given in this area; the other titles are given in a contents note.

Physical description area. Rule 2.5B8 gives several options on treating complex paging. The first method was chosen. The page numbers were added and qualified with "in various pagings." AACR 1 would have required placing the page numbers in brackets because they are not taken directly from the last page of each sequence. The previous rules also allowed the treatment chosen by LC.

Note area. All the items are facsimile reprints of the originals, which is not apparent from the publication dates of the contents note; therefore an explanatory note was added. The contents are given in full as required under Rule 21.1B2. The author statement was added to the third title since it appeared on the original title page. None of the other titles had an author statement on the original title page or in the text itself.

Access points:

Main entry. The title main entry was derived according to Rule 21.1C2, since this is a collection of plays.

Added entries. An added entry, author and title, was provided for the original work (Rule 21.10) and also for the only other named author and title. The second added entry is an analytical (Rule 13.4) since the work is contained in the item. The first two versions are adaptations by Devenant-Dryden according to the introduction and the last title is attributed to David Garrick, although his authorship is doubtful. We decided to follow LC's example and make an added entry for the libretto under the composer, since he is prominently named on the original title page (not shown here) and the work is only attributed to David Garrick. AACR 2 does not require the language after "Libretto" if the text is in the original (Rule 25.5D). The date of the reprint was added to all added entries according to Rule 25.5C, which permits one to add data to distinguish the uniform titles.

Example M18 (Monograph): Analytic to Monographic Series (Compare with Example S10)

> Berry, Mary Frances.
>   Stability, security, and continuity [text] :
> Mr. Justice Burton and decision-making in the
> Supreme Court, 1945-1958 / Mary Frances Berry.
> -- Westport, Conn. : Greenwood Press, 1978.
>   viii, 286 p. : ports. ; 22 cm. -- (Contributions
> in legal studies, ISSN 0147-1074 ; no 1)
>   Bibliography: p. [269]-277.
>   Includes index.
>
>   I. Title

Pre-AACR 2

> Berry, Mary Frances.
>   Stability, security, and continuity : Mr. Justice
> Burton and decision-making in the Supreme Court,
> 1945-1958 / Mary Frances Berry. -- Westport, Conn. :
> Greenwood Press, 1978.
>   viii, 286 p. : ill. ; 22 cm. -- (Contributions
> in legal studies ; no. 1 ISSN 0147-1074)
>   Bibliography: p. [269]-277.
>   Includes index.
>
>   I. Title.

(LC copy; AACR 1, Chapter 6, revised)

Discussion

Description:

General statement. The AACR 2 record illustrates the similarity to applications under Chapter 6, revised. The two records differ only in the position of the ISSN in the series statement.

Series area. In Chapter 6, revised, the ISSN is simply tacked onto the series statement, directly after the volume designation. AACR 2 places it in a more logical position, particularly in terms of machine filing and access. It precedes the series volume designation and is separated from any foregoing data by a comma.

Access points:

Main entry. The main entry is the personal author (Rule 21.1A1).

Added entries. The title and the series will be additional access points for this work. The first access point is provided for by Rule 21.30J. The series access is via the monographic series cataloged as a main entry series with its own bibliographic description (Rule 13.2). It is, of course, possible to make a separate added entry for the series statement, but that decision should be made in accord with an individual library's policy.

Example M19A & 19B (Monograph): "With" (AACR 2) or "Bound With" or "Issued With" (Pre-AACR 2)

> Nelson, Theodor H.
>   Computer lib [text] : you can and must understand
> computers now / [Theodor H. Nelson]. -- 1st ed. --
> [Chicago?] : T.H. Nelson ; Chicago (Box 2622, Chicago,
> Ill. 60690) : Hugo's Book Service [distributor], 1974.
>   69 p. : ill. ; 36 cm.
>   Cover title.
>   Includes bibliographical references.
>   With: Dream machines / Theodor H. Nelson. [Chicago?]:
> T.H. Nelson, 1974.
>
>   I. Title.

> Nelson, Theodor H.
>   Dream machines [text] : new freedoms through computer
> screens : a minority report / [Theodor H. Nelson]. --
> [Chicago?] : T.H. Nelson ; Chicago (Box 2622, Chicago,
> Ill. 60690) : Hugo's Book Service [distributor], 1974.
>   DM 59 p. : ill. ; 36 cm.
>   Cover title.
>   Pages also numbered 70-127, inversely.
>   With: Computer lib / Theodor H. Nelson. [Chicago?] :
> T.H. Nelson, 1974.
>
>   I. Title.

Pre-AACR 2

> Nelson, Theodor H.
>   Computer lib / you can and must understand computers
> now / [Theodor H. Nelson]. -- 1st ed. -- [Chicago] :
> Nelson : [available] from Hugo's Book Service, 1974.
>   69 p. : ill. ; 36 cm.

Cover title.
Includes bibliographical references.
Issued with the author's Dream machines. Chicago, 1974.

I. Title.

Nelson, Theodor H.
Dream machines : new freedoms through computer screens --a minority report / [Theodor H. Nelson]. -- [Chicago] : Nelson : [available from Hugo's Book Service, 1974.]
DM 59 p. : ill. ; 36 cm.
Issued with the author's Computer lib. Chicago, 1974.
Pages also numbered 70-127, inversely.
Includes bibliographical references.

I. Title.

(LC copy, both records; AACR 1, Chapter 6, revised)

Discussion

Description:

Chief sources of information. The item is a paperback edition and the title page is also the cover. As the example shows, the author's name appears only on page two, next to the copyright; therefore, it was given in brackets in the statement of responsibility. We must remember that AACR 2 is very specific about sources of information and how the data is presented in the description. Whenever information transcribed in the bibliographic record is not taken from the chief source of information it must be placed in square brackets.

Title and statement of responsibility area. The first AACR 2 record is identical to the one transcribed according to Chapter 6, revised. Both are based on the ISBD guidelines, only the GMD (general material designation) has been added to the AACR 2 record. However, the AACR 2 for the second title, Dream Machines, differs somewhat. Here it is probably a matter of interpretation of the rules and we decided to make the phrase "a minority report" into a subsequent "other title information" and to drop the long dash from the transcription.

Edition area. Only the first title of the "bound with" has the edition statement on the title page, as can be verified by the sample title pages and the imprint data. The option to add an edition statement, given in Rule 1.2B4, was not selected since it did not really apply in this case. We are dealing here with a first edition; this is generally implied when an edition statement indicating otherwise is lacking.

Publication, distribution, etc. area. We chose to treat the author as the publisher, to guess at the place of publication and to add the full address of the distributor. This appears particularly useful for private publications. The rules do not deal with a situation of this type, when the probable place of publication is the same as that of the distributor. We decided to repeat the distributor's location and to add the address since no major trade publisher is involved.

This statement exemplifies three changes in the transcription of the imprint: (1) when the author is also the publisher, any initials are given with the personal name (1.4D4); (2) when the publisher or distributor is obscure, the full address may be given in the imprint (1.4C7); and (3) when the function of the distributor is not clear in the imprint, the word describing the function may be added (1.4E1).

Physical description area. The pagination of this item is complex. The volume is continuously paged, as recorded in the note area for *Dream Machines*. That title, however, also has its own pagination and each numeral is preceded by the abbreviation "DM" (Dream Machines). AACR 2 Rule 2.5B14 was applied to resolve the problem, although the rule addresses the instance when ". . . a volume has pagination of its own and also bears the pagination of a larger work of which it is a part. . . ." In this case *Dream Machines* and *Computer Lib* are interdependent. Applying the above rule, the last numbered page of each title is recorded in the respective extent of item element, and the *Dream Machines* record contains the full pagination data in the note area.

Note area. "Bound with," "With, as issued," or "Issued with" are no longer used in AACR 2. The new rules do not differentiate these terms and simply use the designation "With" in all cases. The rather free form of the note in the Pre-AACR 2 record has become a formal note. The word "With" is followed by a colon (:) and the information about the other title is transcribed in the same manner as the title and statement of responsibility area. The imprint information is also given in a formalized style using prescribed punctuation; only the space-dash-space (--) does not precede the place of publication (1.7A3, "Form of notes. Order of information").

Access points:

Main entry. The choice for main entry is simply the author of either title (Rule 21.1A2).

Added entries. The only added access required for each record is the title proper (21.30J).

Example M20 (Monograph): Card Format

```
            [Piagetian inventories [text] : the experiments of Jean
                Piaget / Centre for Educational Research and Inno-
                vation]. -- [Paris] : OECD, [1977].
                ca. 250 cards ; 13 x 20 cm. + 1 guide (109 p. ;
            20 cm.)
                Title from container.

            I.  Piaget, Jean, 1896-   . II.  Centre for Educational
            Research and Innovation. III.  Organisation for Economic
            Co-operation and Development.
```

Pre-AACR 2

Centre for Educational Research and Innovation.
   Piagetian inventories : the experiments of Jean
Piaget / Centre for Educational Research and Inno-
vation. -- [Paris] : Organization for Economic
Co-operation and Development, 197-?.
   ca. 250 cards in box ; 14 x 23 cm.
   Includes booklet.

I. Piaget, Jean, 1896-   . II. Organization for
Economic Co-operation and Development. III. Title.

(not LC copy; AACR 1, Chapter 6, revised)

Discussion

Description:

Title and statement of responsibility area. The three elements which constitute this area
are placed in square brackets since the title page, the chief source of information for monographs, is lacking. The first note indicates that the title was transcribed from the container.

Publication, distribution, etc. area. The place and the date are each within its own set
of brackets, since the information comes from the accompanying guide and not from the
item itself. Even though the full name of the publisher appears on the container, the briefest
form (also on the container) was given. The acronym is internationally understood and identifiable and thus should be used according to Rule 1.4D2.

Physical description area. This area is problematic. The rules of Chapter 2 (Books,
Pamphlets, etc.) do not offer a solution for cards. Rule 2.5 deals only with pages and leaves,
columns and sheets, volumes, cases or portfolios, etc. In order to catalog this item, some im-
provising is necessary. The parallel rules for microforms were examined and then the decision to describe the cards and give their size was made.
   The guide to the *Inventories* was treated as accompanying material and added after the
plus sign (+). The physical description was taken from the rules for monographs, as required by AACR 2, Rule 1.5E1, optional addition.

Note area. The note identifying the source of the title information is adopted from the
microform format, as is some of the physical description (i.e., the extent of item). Chapter 2
prescribes use of the term "case(s)" or "portfolio(s)" which was not satisfactory in this instance.

Access points:

Main entry. Rule 21.1C requires that the item be entered under its title when it is a
work that ". . . emanates from a corporate body but does not fall into one or more of the
categories given in 21.1B2 and is not of personal authorship."

Added entries. The rules under 21.20 provide for an access point under the corporate body if it is prominently named. This applies to the OECD and the Centre. The prominence of Piaget and his relationship to the content of the work justify an added entry under his name as provided by 21.30F, "Other related persons or bodies."

Example M21 (Monograph): Accompanying Material / Slides

> Furstenberg, Jean, 1890-
> Le grand siècle en France et ses bibliophiles [text] : volumes à provenance, manuscrits et documents de la Fondation Furstenberg-Beaumesnil et de la Collection Jean et Eugénie Furstenberg / Jean Furstenberg. -- Hamburg : E. Hauswedell, 1972.
> 158 p. : ill. ; 29 cm. + 60 slides (col. ; 5 x 5 cm.)
> Summary in English and German.
> "Présentation générale par Richard von Sichowsky." -- Colophon.
> Slides in pockets.
> ISBN 3-7762-0027-8.
>
> I. Sichowsky, Richard von, ed. II. Fondation Furstenberg-Beaumesnil. III. Title.

Pre-AACR 2

> Furstenberg, Jean, 1890-
> Le grand siècle en France et ses bibliophiles. Volumes à provenance, manuscrits et documents de la Fondation Furstenberg-Beaumesnil et de la Collection Jean et Eugénie Furstenberg. Hamburg, E. Hauswedell, 1972.
> 158 p. illus., 60 col. slides (2 x 2 in. in pockets) 29 cm.
> Summary in English and French.
> "Présentation générale par Richard von Sichowsky."
>
> I. Fondation Furstenberg-Beaumesnil. II. Sichowsky, Richard von, ed. III. Title.

(LC copy)

Discussion

Description:

Title and statement of responsibility area. Following AACR 2 Rule 1.1F3, the statement of responsibility was transcribed in its proper position as the third element of the area. AACR 1, of course, allowed for omitting the author when the same as the main entry heading.

Publication, distribution, etc. area. This area is identical in content to the AACR 1 record, with the exception of the punctuation, since all data required are on the title page.

Physical description area. Here the two records vary widely. AACR 2 presents the physical description of the item in two distinct areas. The earlier record mixes the physical description of the two formats in the publication. The physical description of the slides is given according to the rules relating to this format (8.5C12 and 8.5D5).

Note area. The arrangement of the notes follows the sequence in which the areas they relate to appear in the record. There are two additions to the AACR 2 notes: location of the slides in relation to the main work and the ISBN. The quoted note has the source appended; it is a requirement of AACR 2. However, give the source of the quotation if it is transcribed from the chief source of information (1.7A3, "Quotations").

Access points:

Main entry. The main entry is under the personal name according to Rule 21.1A2.

Added entries. Although the editor's name does not appear on the title page, his name is given in the note since the publication followed an older practice of giving the author, title and publisher in the colophon. Consequently an added entry, or access point, was provided for the name of the editor, and the function qualifier was added. Since the foundation appears prominently on the title page and in the other title information, an added entry was provided by applying Rule 21.30E. The title is also given as an access point (Rule 21.30J).

Example M22 (Monograph): Accompanying Material / Sound Recording (Disc)

> Dobson, Rosemary.
>   Rosemary Dobson reads from her own work [text]. --
> St. Lucia, Qld. : University of Queensland Press,
> 1970.
>   16 p. ; 20 cm. + 1 sound disc ((ca. 20 min.) :
> 45 rpm). -- (Poets on record ; 2)
>   Sound disc in pocket.
>   Selected bibliography: p. 15-16.
>
>   I. Title.

Pre-AACR 2

> Dobson, Rosemary.
>   Rosemary Dobson reads from her own work.
> [St. Lucia] University of Queensland Press
> [Distributed by International Scholarly
> Book Services, 1970]
>   16 p. and phonodisc (2 s. 7 in. 45 rpm) in
> pocket. 20 cm. (Poets on record, 2)
>   Bibliography: p. 15-16.
>
>   I. Title.

(LC copy)

Discussion

Description:

Title and statement of responsibility area. The title includes the statement of responsibility which is transcribed according to Rule 1.1B2. The statement cannot be transposed to its proper position, as required by 1.1F2, not only because a case ending is affected but also because the title would have become unintelligible.

Publication, distribution, etc. area. The AACR 2 imprint data lacks all square brackets, since the source of information has been expanded to "other preliminaries and the colophon." The place is identified by the province. (Its abbreviation is given in Appendix B.14.) AACR 2 contains a substantially expanded list of abbreviations for place names which must be used when a location needs further identification. Althouh AACR 1 also suggests the identification of a place name, if that is necessary, in this case the librarian may have decided that this was not necessary since it could be inferred from the university's name. However, in this instance we decided not to follow the LC example.

Physical description area. This area exhibits the greatest changes. In AACR 2 the elements describing the physical aspects of the item come first and the accompanying materials' physical description may be added after the plus (+) sign, as in the example. Analogous to AACR 1 the physical description of the accompanying materials follows the rules of the type or format of the material (see Rule 6.5 for sound recordings). The location of the accompanying material is given in the note area.

Access points:

Main entry. The main entry is, according to Rule 21.1A, the person responsible for the content of the work. This would also apply to the sound recording; the performer generally is treated as an added entry. Here the performer is also the main entry heading, so an added entry is unnecessary.

Added entries. In this case the title becomes an added access point.

Example M23 (Monograph): Accompanying Material / Sound Recording (Cassette)

> Erickson, Milton H.
>   Hypnotic realities [text] : the induction of clinical
> hypnosis and forms of indirect suggestion / by
> Milton H. Erickson, Ernest L. Rossi, Sheila I. Rossi ;
> with a foreword by André M. Weitzenhoffer. -- New York :
> Irvington Publishers : Distributed by Halsted Press, 1976.
>   xix, 326 p. ; 24 cm. + 1 cassette.
>   Bibliography: p. 315-318.
>   Includes index.
>   ISBN 0-470-15169-2.

I. Rossi, Ernest L. II. Rossi, Sheila I.
III. Title.

Pre-AACR 2

Erickson, Milton H.
   Hypnotic realities : the induction of clinical
hypnosis and forms of indirect suggestion / by
Milton H. Erickson, Ernest L. Rossi, Sheila I.
Rossi ; with a foreword by André M. Weitzenhoffer.
-- New York : Irvington Publishers : distributed
by Halsted Press, c1976.
   xix, 326 p. ; 24 cm. & cassette.
   Bibliography: p. 315-318.
   Includes index.
   ISBN 0-470-1569-2.

   I. Rossi, Ernest Lawrence, joint author.
   II. Rossi, Sheila I., joint author. III. Title.

(LC copy, AACR 1, Chapter 6, revised)

Discussion

Description:

General statement. The differences between these two records are mainly in punctuation since the second record is cataloged according to Chapter 6, revised, of AACR 1; i.e., it is an ISBD (M) record.

Publication, distribution, etc. area. The first difference is in the imprint area. AACR 2 requires the capitalization of the first word in the publisher, distributor, etc. area, when that word is ". . . not an integral part of the name of place, publisher, distributor, manufacturer, etc. . . ." (see Appendix A.7B).

Physical description area. The second difference is in the extent of item area, where under Chapter 6, revised, an ampersand (&) is used instead of the " + " and where now the number of items is specified, even if there is only one accompanying item, as in this example. Rule 1.5E, which treats accompanying material, gives the cataloger four choices of description and an optional addition. The description may be very brief, as the one above, or more detailed, as in other examples for accompanying material. The detailed description of the accompanying material follows the rules of the chapter which deals with its physical form. In this case more precise data is not available.

Access points:

Main entry. The main entry is under the first author named, when there are two or more names in the statement of responsibility and principal responsibility is not indicated (Rule 21.6C1).

Added entries. Added entries are provided for the names of the collaborators (Rule 21.30B, "Collaborators"). The function designator "joint author" is not applied in AACR 2. A title added entry is always provided for a work entered under a name (21.30J).

MUSIC

Music is one format that must make a large leap into the present and conform to ISBD form employed in AACR 2. A specific ISBD format for music is not yet available; it will be the "ISBD(PM)" (printed music). However, the ISBD(G) (general) is the foundation on which all ISBDs are built and was used by the writers of AACR 2, who have, one hopes, formulated rules that will be compatible with the forthcoming ISBD(PM).

The four examples in this chapter present only a very small fraction of the types of printed music available. The intent is to demonstrate the AACR 2 format and not to give examples of the large variety of items found in a music catalog or collection. The examples also illustrate the uniform titles and the changes in choice and form of access for this group of materials.

Title and Statement of Responsibility

The descriptive rules for music in AACR 1 draw heavily on AACR 1, Chapter 6, for monographs, just as AACR 2, Chapter 5 (Music) refers to the details in Chapter 1 (General Rules). However, when the materials differ special rules are provided. While AACR 1 and AACR 2 both accept the "list" title page ("a list of titles including the title being cataloged") as a source of information, AACR 2 is more specific and helpful for the generalist. The old rules consider the medium of performance, opus number and key, but do not illustrate their application. With AACR 2, even the individual without a good music background should be able to understand and apply the rules.

Other AACR 2 rules refer to AACR 2 Chapter 1, just as AACR 1 Rule 244C refers to the corresponding Rule 133C, to resolve a multilanguage title page problem. Example MU4 illustrates such a problem and shows how it is solved by applying either AACR 1 or AACR 2 rules. Note that the composers in Examples MU2-MU4 are also repeated in the statement of responsibility in compliance with AACR 2 (Rule 1.1F1), although they are the main entry; in the pre-AACR 2 record they were legitimately omitted.

The GMD (general material designation) is present in each example. A general library may find that it is a very useful designation for the library user; in a special music library it will be less helpful.

Publication, Distribution, etc.

As with monographs the distributor information may also be recorded for music and, if beneficial, so may the date of distribution appearing in the item. Plate and publishers' numbers are no longer recorded in the imprint area but are given in the notes (see Rule 5.4D2). Lack of place of publication and/or publisher are indicated as for monographs (see Rules 1.4C6 and 1.4D6). As previously stated, the specifics of a rule will not be repeated from the general rules if the latter also apply to the individual format. Only a general reference to all the rules applying to an element of the area will be given.

Physical Description

The physical description area has few changes, the most noticeable one being that a general material designation must be given. It may be as general as the term "music" when none of the specific designations enumerated under Rule 5.5B1 apply. The term "music" may be omitted, however, when the GMD is in the title and statement of responsibility area (see Examples MU1 and MU2). In addition, the number of physical units of an item is always given, even though there may only be one. AACR 1 (Rule 246B1) permitted the omission of the number if there was only one piece. Other AACR 2 changes in dimension, illustration or accompanying material are those of AACR 2 Chapter 1.

Series Area

The series area rules do not differ from those for monographs or from the general rules. The original AACR 1 rules also referred to the monograph rules for specific instructions.

Notes

Changes were also made in the note area. AACR 1 Rules 248A and 248B were combined; the term "species" was changed to "form of composition," which can be interpreted more easily. Rule 5.7B1 makes no references to the uniform title as did Rule 248B. The authors of the new code thus maintained their clear-cut division between description and access points.

As explained in the discussion of changes in the publication, distribution, etc., area, the plate and publishers' numbers are now given in the notes. "Publisher's number" is no longer abbreviated as "Pub. no." but as "Publisher's no.:". The plate number designation is abbreviated in the same manner as before, but now the colon (:) follows it. When the music volume is a reprint that information, along with publisher's or plate number, is transcribed in the note area.

As stated under monographs, the "dashed" entry has disappeared from the record. Under AACR 1 Rule 246C, an additional copy necessary for the performance could be indicated as: _____ _____ Copy 2. (The first long dash represented the author's/composer's name and the second the title.) Under AACR 2 Rule 5.7B20, the note would only state that the library holds two copies of the score (e.g., "Library has 2 copies.").

The new rules also provide for the ISBN, its terms of availability and qualifications such as volume number or type of binding.

EXAMPLE MU1

Verso of Title Page

Title Page

NEW CATHOLIC HYMNAL

COMPILED AND EDITED
BY
ANTHONY PETTI
AND
GEOFFREY LAYCOCK

CONGREGATION EDITION

, 1971

don
lbourne
, Toronto

ST. MARTIN'S PRESS
NEW YORK

EXAMPLE MU2

EARLIER AMERICAN MUSIC
EDITED BY H. WILEY HITCHCOCK
for the *Music Library Association*

8

Title Page

EDWARD MACDOWELL

PIANO PIECES
(Opp. 51, 55, 61, 62)

INTRODUCTION BY H. WILEY HITCHCOCK
Director, Institute for Studies in American Music,
Brooklyn College, CUNY

This Da Capo Press edition of Edward MacDowell's
Piano Pieces cumulates four collections of MacDowell's
piano music (Opp. 51, 55, 61, 62) published originally
between 1896 and 1902.

Library of Congress Catalog Card Number 70-170391
ISBN 0-306-77308-2

Copyright © 1972 by the Music Library Association

Published by Da Capo Press, Inc.
A Subsidiary of Plenum Publishing Corporation
227 West 17th Street, New York, New York 10011

DA CAPO PRESS • NEW YORK • 1972

Verso of Title Page

Title Page

Dimitri Schostakowitsch

Die Nase

Oper in drei Akten und einem Epilog

Text vom Komponisten nach der Novelle von Gogol
Deutsche Übertragung von Helmut Wagner und Karl Heinz Füssl

Klavierauszug
von
Karl Götz

Ausgabe nur für
Bühnenzwecke

UNIVERSAL EDITION

First Page of Music / Imprint Date

> > ↗ cresc.
Alle Rechte vorbehalten
© Copyright 1962 by Universal Edition A. G., Wien   Universal Edition Nr. 13439

**Left-Hand
Title Page**

Elegy for Young Lovers

Opera in three acts by
Wystan H. Auden and Chester Kallman

Music by
Hans Werner Henze

**Right-Hand
Title Page**

Elegie für junge Liebende

Oper in drei Akten von
Wystan H. Auden und Chester Kallman

Musik von
Hans Werner Henze

Deutsche Fassung von Ludwig Landgraf
unter Mitarbeit von Werner Schachteli und dem Komponisten

Studien-Partitur
Edition Schott 5040

B. SCHOT

Schott & Co. Ltd., Lon
Schott Music Cor

First Page of Music

by B. Schott's Söhne 1961

B. SCHOTT'S SÖHNE · MAINZ
Schott & Co. Ltd., London · B. Schott's Söhne (Editions Max Eschig), Paris
Schott Music Corp. (Associated Music Publishers Inc.), New York

Example MU1 (Music): Vocal Score

> New Catholic hymnal [music] / compiled and
>   edited by Anthony Petti and Geoffrey Laycock.
>   -- Congregation ed. -- New York : St. Martin's
>   Press, 1971.
>   Unaac. melodies (xvii, 250 p.) ; 22 cm.
>
> I. Petti, Anthony, comp. II. Laycock, Geoffrey,
> comp.

Pre-AACR 2

> Petti, Anthony, comp.
>   New Catholic hymnal. Compiled and edited
> by Anthony Petti and Geoffrey Laycock. Congre-
> gation ed. New York, St. Martin's Press [1971]
>   xii, 250 p. 22 cm.
>   Unaac. melodies.
>
> I. Laycock, Geoffrey, comp. II. Title.

(LC copy)

Discussion

Description:

Title and statement of responsibility area. The data transcribed in this area are taken from the chief source of information, the title page. The differences between the two records are in the prescribed punctuation and the material designation.

Edition area. There are no differences in this area.

Publication, distribution, etc. area. The expanded sources for the transcription of data affect this area; however, the difference is in appearance and not in content. Brackets do not need to be added to a date under AACR 2 rules when it is taken from a source other than the title page but is still found in one of the prescribed sources.

Physical description area. AACR 2 permits the inclusion of the "specific material designation" (i.e., a term or terms which state the class of material to which an item belongs) in this area. The rules give a number of specific terms (Rule 5.5B1), but none applied here. The other options also did not add to the specificity we could gain for this area under AACR 2; therefore we chose to apply the term "unaccompanied melodies," which is the first note of the pre-AACR 2 record, and then added extent of item information and the size.

Access points:

Main entry. Main entry is under the title of the work according to Rule 21.7A2. Rule

21.39A1, concerning liturgical works, could not be applied to this title, since the title does not conform to the definition for liturgical works, which are treated under 21.39.

Added entries. Added entries are made for compilers of a work according to Rule 21.30D. The function designator option was taken and the abbreviation "comp." added.

Example MU2 (Music): Piano Selections

> MacDowell, Edward.
>   [Piano music. Selections]
>   Piano pieces [music] : (Opp. 51, 55, 61, 62) /
> Edward MacDowell ; introd. H. Wiley Hitchcock.
> -- New York : Da Capo Press, 1972.
>   144 p. ; 28 cm. -- (Earlier American music ;
> 8)
>   ". . . Piano pieces cumulates four collections of
> MacDowell's piano music (Opp. 51, 55, 61, 62)
> published originally between 1896-1902." --
> T.p. verso.
>   Contents: Woodland sketches (Op. 51, 1896) --
> Sea pieces (Op. 55, 1898) -- Fireside tales (Op.
> 61, 1902) -- New England idyls (Op. 62, 1902).
>   ISBN 0-306-77308-2.
>
>   I. Title.

Pre-AACR 2

> MacDowell, Edward Alexander, 1861-1908.
>   [Works, piano. Selections]
>   Piano pieces (Opp. 51, 52, 61, 62). Introd.
> by H. Wiley Hitchcock. New York, Da Capo Press,
> 1972.
>   144 p. 29 cm. (Earlier American music, 8)

(LC copy)

Discussion

Description:

Title and statement of responsibility area. The chief source of information is the title page. Contrary to the title transcription in the pre-AACR 2 record, "Piano Pieces" alone is treated as the title proper and "(Opp. 51, . . .)" etc. as the other title information. The first indicates that we are dealing with a collection of piano pieces and the second specifies the individual works contained in the collection. Rule 5.1B2 (adding opus number to title proper) could not be applied since we are dealing with a collection and not a specific musical piece. The general material designation is given even though it seems redundant in relation to the uniform title, which also includes "music," but once the decision has been made to employ the GMD it should always be added to a record. The composer's name appears as the specified element in the statement of responsibility. The introduction is treated as a secondary statement of responsibility and is the last element of the area.

Publication, distribution, etc. area. This area differs only in the prescribed punctuation and its accompanying spacing.

Physical description area. A specific material designation was not added; Rule 5.5B1 allows the word "music" to be added in this area " . . . unless a general material designation appears in the description . . ." Thus the area differs only in the spacing and punctuation but not in content.

Note area. Two types of notes were added: an edition history note indicating a reprint and a contents note. The contents were transcribed as they appeared in the table of contents including the opus number and the date of publication. Rule 5.7B18 permits the addition of the opus number if it adds to the identification of the piece. We felt this applied here.

Access points:

Main entry. The definition of personal author given under Rule 21.1A1 applies and entry under the author's name (Rule 21.1A2) is the next logical step.

Added entries. A title added entry is not provided since Rule 21.30J4 explicitly states not to make an added entry when a conventionalized uniform title has been used for a musical work.

Uniform title:

The uniform title was derived by applying Rule 25.36A, "Works of various types in one specific medium." (Since "pieces" is a very general term we chose "piano music.") The second part was chosen by employing Rule 25.36C, which requires the term "selections" to be added to the first part of the uniform title when a collection does not contain all the works of a given type.

Example MU3 (Music): Vocal Score / German Translation

> Shostakovich, Dmitri.
>   [Nos. Vocal score. German]
>   Die Nase [music] : Oper in drei Akten und einem
> Epilog ; Dimitri Schostakowitsch ; Text vom Kom-
> ponisten nach der Novelle von Gogol ; deutsche
> Übertragung von Helmut Wagner und Karl Heinz Füssl ;
> Klavierauszug von Karl Götz. -- Ausg. nur für
> Bühnenzwecke. -- Wien : Universal Edition, c1962.
>   1 vocal score (396 p.) : 31 cm. -- (Universal
> Edition ; Nr. 13439)
>
>   I. Gogol, Nicolai. Nos.

Pre-AACR 2

> Shostakovich, Dmitriĭ Dmitrievich, 1906-1975.
>   [The nose. Piano-vocal score. German]
>   Die Nase; Oper in 3 Akten und einem Epilog. Text
> vom Komponisten nach der Novelle von Gogol. Deutsche
> Übertragung von Helmut Wagner und Karl Heinz Füssl.
> Klavierauszug von Karl Götz. Ausg. nur für Bühnen-
> zwecke. [Wien] Universal Edition [c1962]
>   396 p. 31 cm. (Universal Edition, Nr. 13439)
>
>   I. Title.

(LC copy)

Discussion

Description:

Title and statement of responsibility area. The title page, as the chief source of information for the bibliographic transcription, provides all the necessary data to describe the item.
The GMD (general material designation), which we opted to apply, is the only interpolated
data in this first area. The differences between the two records are the punctuation, the spacing and the German form of the composer's name as it appears on the title page.

Edition area. The statement "edition for stage use only" (translation of "Ausgabe nur
für Bühnenzwecke") is an edition statement and is separated from the preceding area by the
appropriate prescribed punctuation.

Publication, distribution, etc. area. This statement matches that of the pre-AACR 2
record except that it omits the brackets. The expansion of the sources of information for this
area, beyond the limitation to the title page, here makes it unnecessary to use brackets for
data not taken from the chief source of information.

Physical description area. Here the record exhibits a greater change than in the other
areas. The "specific material designation" and the number of pieces (i.e., physical items) are
recorded as the first part of the area. Then follow the statement of extent of the item (the
pagination, see Rules 5.5B1 and 5.5B2) and the dimensions. In this example the uniform title
qualifier and the "specific material designation" are identical. Since we have made the decision to use the GMD, both appear in the record.

Access points:

Main entry. The main entry is the composer's name. In the case of a name in a non-
roman language the established English-language form is used (Rule 22.3C1) and not
necessarily the form that appears on the title page. The very specific rule for "musical works
that include words" (Rule 21.19) applies in this instance. An added entry for the author and

title on which this work is based is required by the same rule; AACR 1 and the old *ALA Cataloging Rules for Author and Title Entries* (the *Red Book*) had the same requirements. (A cataloger's oversight could be the only reason for not having an author and title entry for Gogol and *The Nose* in the pre-AACR 2 record.)

Added entries. A title added entry is not required since a conventionalized uniform title has been used in the entry (see Rule 21.30J 4). As noted earlier, an author/title added entry is made for the original work on which the opera is based.

Uniform title:

The uniform title was given as an example rather than a requirement. Rule 25.1 states that the use of a uniform title is a matter of local policy. We arrived at this title by applying Rules 25.27A ("Use as the basis for a uniform title the composer's title in the original language, etc."); 25.31B3 (the item is a vocal score with an accompanying piano arrangement); and 25.31B7 (the libretto is the German translation of the original Russian). As the basic rule for uniform title states, the uniform title is used to bring together in one area of the catalog all "manifestations" of the same work and to distinguish one title of the work from the other. Note that the term "Piano-vocal score" is not applied in AACR 2; "vocal score" in the physical description area implies that the item contains all vocal parts of the work and that the accompanying arrangement is for the keyboard (see "Vocal score," AACR 2 Glossary, p. 572).

Example MU4 (Music): Miniature Score & Parallel Text

> Henze, Hans Werner.
>   [Elegie für junge Liebende. English & German]
>   Elegie für junge Liebende [music] : Oper in drei
> Akten / von Wystan H. Auden und Chester Kallman ;
> Musik von Hans Werner Henze ; deutsche Fassung von
> Ludwig Landgraf unter Mitarbeit von Werner
> Schachteli und dem Komponisten = Elegy for young
> lovers : opera in three acts / by Wystan H. Auden
> and Chester Kallman ; music by Hans Werner Henze.
> -- Mainz : B. Schott's Söhne ; New York : Schott
> Music Corp. (Associated Music Publishers), 1961.
>   1 miniature score (532 p.) ; 28 cm. -- (Edition
> Schott ; 5040)
>   "The opera was commissioned by the Süddeutscher
> Rundfunk, Stuttgart." -- Prelim.
>
>   I. Auden, Wystan H. II. Kallman, Chester E.
> III. Title: Elegy for young lovers.

Pre-AACR 2

> Henze, Hans Werner, 1923-
>   [Elegie für junge Liebende. English & German]
>   Elegie für junge Liebende; Oper in drei Akten von
> Wystan H. Auden und Chester Kallman. Musik von Hans

Werner Henze. Deutsche Fassung von Ludwig Landgraf
unter Mitarbeit von Werner Schachteli und dem Komponisten. Elegy for young lovers. Mainz, B.
Schott's Söhne; New York, Schott Music Corp. (Associated Music Publishers) [1961]
    1 miniature score (532 p.) 28 cm. (Edition
Schott, 5040)

    I. Auden, Wystan Hugh, 1907-   . Elegy for young
lovers. II. Kallman, Chester, 1921-   . Elegy
for young lovers. III. Title: Elegy for young
lovers.

(not LC copy)

Discussion

Description:

Chief sources of information. The item displays two title pages, one in German and a
second in English. The rules which apply for the selection of a chief source of information
in the example lead us from Rule 5.0B1 (chief source of information for music) to Rule
5.0H (items with several chief sources of information), and then back to Chapter 1, Rule
1.0H (basic rule for item with several chief sources of information). We applied Rule
1.0H 4, b, and chose the German title page as the main source of information with the data
from the English title page as parallel title, etc., information. In arriving at our decision we
considered the musical form of the work (opera) and consulted several non-German-language
reference sources to determine how the work is cited consistently. We found it under the
German title followed by the English one in parentheses. With this knowledge we chose the
German-language title page for our chief source of information. The choice for the pre-
AACR 2 record was based on the same concept; that is, Rule 3.4B5 ("the aspect in which
the work is to be treated") in the *LC Descriptive Cataloging Rules* (the *Green Book*).

Title and statement of responsibility area. The data for this area are transcribed
systematically as on the title page. After the German-language information has been
transcribed, the English-language information is treated as parallel title and statement of
responsibility (Rules 1.1D, 1.1F, etc.); the GMD was added according to Rule 5.1C. This is
an example of the specific format rules referring back to the basic rules in Chapter 1.

Publication, distribution, etc. area. Both records exhibit identical information. The
foreign and North American publishers are given, as well as the date. Again the difference is
the prescribed punctuation and spacing.

Physical description area. The instructions for the information in this area also have affected their physical appearance, not their contents. There is one difference in these rules:
formerly a single score was not indicated by a "1"; the current rules require that we always
state the number of physical pieces (or units) (see Rule 5.5B1).

Access points:

Main entry. The main entry is according to Rule 21.19, "Musical works that include words." The added entries for the librettists follow this rule also.

Added entries. Rule 21.19 requires not only an added access point for the author and title on which a work is based (as in the MU3 example), but it also requires access to the librettists.

Uniform title:

The uniform title is derived by applying Rule 25.27A (the composer's original title). Rule 25.31B7 adds specificity to the uniform title by indicating that the work contains also the English and German texts of the opera. The last rule also contains a reference to 25.5D, which gives more detailed instructions for adding a language qualifier to the uniform title. We not only learn when to add the name of a language but also when we may add a second language if the work requires this additional identification. The AACR 1 uniform title is identical; only the rules differ. The AACR 1 instructions for the music uniform title are all found in Chapter 13 (Music).

SOUND RECORDINGS

Title and Statement of Responsibility

In 1976 a revision of AACR 1, Chapter 14 (Sound Recordings) was published. The changes affected the contents but not the form of the entry for discs. ISBD(NBM) (nonbook material) changes were not anticipated since the ISBD(G) had not yet been published, though it had been conceptualized about the time the revised Chapter 14 was issued. These changes were first published in the fall 1975 LC *Cataloging Service Bulletin,* no. 115.

However, the GMD (general material designation) was anticipated as a "generic medium designator" in the term "sound recording." It was either given following the uniform title or, when not part of the record, placed after the title proper. In either location, square brackets surrounded it. Although we present only a small number of examples with which to illustrate the cataloging of sound recordings, these contain enough variety to afford an overall picture of the new format. Including music on sound recordings also illustrates the special relationship between this format and music. This relationship is reflected in the rules of Chapter 6, AACR 2, particularly when transcribing the title proper and when a music title must be composed applying the uniform title rules.

As Examples SR1-SR4 show, the chief source of information is the disc label. The earlier rule (AACR 1 252B) gave two options—the disc label, or the cover of the album or any container which enclosed the item—with no preferred choice. The result is diversity of interpretation since the disc may have three variant titles: one on the disc label, another on the front cover and a third on the cover's verso. The implications are obvious when we consider shared data bases and shared bibliographic data: consistency and certainty of access cannot be achieved. AACR 2's instructions for chief source will result in greater consistency in the choice of the title proper and retrievability of a title.

The transcription of the title proper follows Rule 1.1B. When the item is recorded music and the title is a generic (e.g., concerto, symphony, quartet), Rule 6.1B2 refers to its parallel in Chapter 5. These rules are correlated with those for music uniform title (25.26-25.36). In AACR 1, Chapter 14, both original and revised, separate entries were made for works lacking a collective title. The change in AACR 2 (Rule 6.1G) brings the treatment of sound recordings closer to that of monographs but still provides the option of separate entries for each work. The provision for transcribing performers is found in two places: the statement of responsibility (Rule 6.1F1) and the note area (Rule 6.7B6). If the performers' responsibility goes beyond that of performing the piece, they may be given in the statement of responsibility and will most likely also become the main entry.

The rules for variant editions of sound recordings were not specifically provided for under AACR 1. The general introduction to AACR 1, Chapter 14 provided the link to AACR 1, Chapter 6, rules for monographs. All rules for the edition area in Chapter 6 applied to sound recordings.

Publication, Distribution, etc.

The publication, distribution, etc. area has been aligned with that of the other formats, and will now always give place of publication, publisher, and date. The publisher's number, preceded by the trade name, is part of the note area. AACR 1 Rule 252C1 requiring only the trade name, serial number and the date has been deleted (see Examples SR1-SR4). The lack of a place of publication and/or publisher is also indicated, according to Rule 1.4, with "[S.n. : s.l.]" (place and publisher are unknown).

Physical Description

One obvious addition in the physical description area is the inclusion of duration (i.e., playing time) in the extent of item. (It was previously given in a note.) The term "cylinder" is replaced by "roll" and is preceded by the term describing the instrument for which it is designed. In addition, "sound" is now the descriptor for each recording type, the exception of course being "roll." However, the term may be omitted if the GMD ([sound recording]) follows the title proper (compare Examples SR3 and SR4). Some new rules have been added to this area; these apply to the type of recording and the gauge for film sound tracks (Rules 6.5C2 and 6.5D3), and to the recording and reproduction characteristics of sound recording (Rule 6.5C8).

Notes

As mentioned in a previous chapter, the order of the notes in AACR 2 has a new sequence, making them easier to learn and apply consistently. This change also occurred for sound recordings. Notes were added as well as deleted. The publisher's number, preceded by the label name, is now found in this area, but the duration has become part of the extent of item.

Series Area

Series rules are the same as for other formats. There are provisions for ISBNs and ISSNs when these are part of the item being cataloged.

EXAMPLE SR1

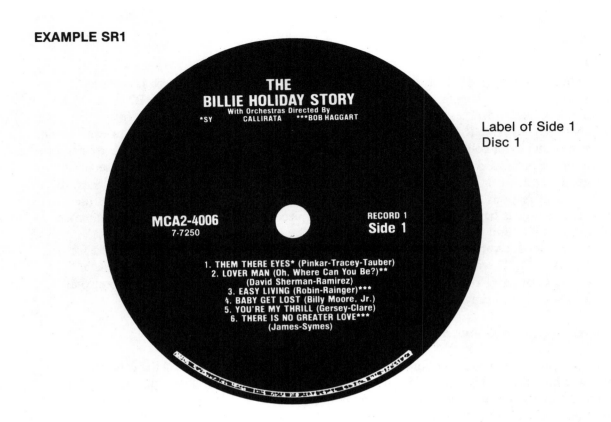

Label of Side 1
Disc 1

EXAMPLE SR2

Label of Side 1
Disc 1

EXAMPLE SR3

Label Side 2

Label Side 1

EXAMPLE SR4

Label Side 1
Disc 1

Example SR1 (Sound Recording): Collection with Collective Title and a Single Performer

>Holiday, Billie, 1915-1959.
>   The Billie Holiday Story [sound recording]. --
>Universal City, Calif. : MCA Records, c1973.
>   2 sound discs : 33 1/3 rpm ; 12 in.
>   Blues and popular songs sung by Billie Holiday
>with orchestras directed by Camarata, Bob Haggart,
>Sy Oliver ; Billy Kyle and his trio.
>   Recorded 1944-1950, previously released as Decca
>DXSB7-161.
>   Contents: Them there eyes -- Lover man -- Easy
>living -- Baby get lost -- You're my thrill -- There
>is no greater love -- That ole devil called love --
>I'll look around -- A pigfoot and a bottle of beer
>-- My man -- Don't explain -- Ain't nobody's business
>if I do -- Deep song -- Crazy he calls me -- Keeps on
>raining -- No more -- Do your duty -- Now or never --
>Good morning heartache -- Somebody's on my mind --
>Porgy -- Solitude -- This is heaven to me -- God
>bless the child.
>   "Notes by William Dufty" on container.
>   MCA2-4006.
>
>I. Title.

Pre-AACR 2

>The Billie Holiday story. [Sound recording] MCA
>   Recordings MCA2-4006. [1973?] p1973.
>   2 discs. 33 1/3 rpm. 12 in.
>   Blues and popular songs, sung by Billie Holiday,
>with various orchestras.
>   Recorded 1944-1950.
>   Previously released by Decca DXSB7-161.
>   Notes by William Dufty on container.
>   Contents: Them there eyes. -- Lover man. -- Easy
>living. -- Baby get lost. -- You're my thrill. --
>There is no greater love. -- That ole devil called love. --
>I'll look around. -- A pigfoot and a bottle of beer. --
>My man. -- Don't explain. -- Ain't nobody's business if
>I do. -- Deep song. -- Crazy he calls me. -- Keeps on
>raining. -- No more. -- Do your duty. -- Now or never. --
>Good morning heartache. -- Somebody's on my mind. --
>Porgy. -- Solitude. -- This is heaven to me. -- God
>bless the child.
>
>I. Holiday, Billie, 1915-1959.

(not LC copy; AACR 1, Chapter 14, revised 1976)

Discussion

Description:

Chief sources of information. The chief source of information for the descriptive data is the disc label, which contained all necessary data to describe the record set.

Title and statement of responsibility area. The title is transcribed as required by Rules 6.1B and 1.1B2; the last rule refers to the statement of responsibility in the title proper. When this rule is applied the statement is not transposed to its prescribed position but it remains part of the title proper. The GMD is the last element in the area; we decided to choose this option since it identifies the medium in the first line of the description.

Rule 6.1F1 requires that the accompanying orchestras, in this instance, be given in the note area (Rule 6.7B6, "Statement of responsibility"). Since the pre-AACR 2 example was cataloged applying the rules of Chapter 14, revised 1976, it also includes a "generic medium designator" (as the GMD is called under these rules); therefore, the two areas look very much alike.

Publication, distribution, etc. area. The information follows the regular format: place, publisher and date. The earlier example only required the publisher, serial identification and the date. As the example shows, rather than having the copyright "c" precede the copyright date, a "p" for pressing is used. The publisher's disc number is given in the note area for the AACR 2 record (Rule 6.7B19).

Note area. The first note relates to the statement of responsibility and gives the accompanying orchestras (Rule 6.7B6). It is followed by the "Edition and history" note (Rule 6.7B7) relating the recording history and the initial Decca release. This is followed by the accompanying material note (Rule 6.7B11) for the information on the container. The contents were given applying Rule 6.7B18; the punctuation separating each title is inferred from the examples in AACR 2 under the rule. Note that in all examples only a long dash (--) separates each title or title and statement of responsibility; there is no period preceding the dash as in the pre-AACR 2 example.

Access points:

Main entry. Rule 21.23C permits entry under the performer when the works performed are by different persons. Under AACR 1 the main entry would be the title (Rule 250B1) with an added entry under the performer (251B).

Added entries. Rule 20.30J requires added access under title when the main entry heading is a personal name.

Example SR2 (Sound Recording): Selections of One Type of Music by One Composer

> Rossini, Gioacchino, 1792-1868.
>   [Overtures. Selections]
>   The Rossini overture album [sound recording]. --
> New York : CBS, 1978.
>   2 discs (69 min.) : 33 1/3 rpm, stereo. ;
> 12 in. -- (Columbia masterworks)
>   Recordings by New York Philharmonic, Leonard Bern-
> stein, conductor ; Cleveland Orchestra, George Szell,
> conductor.
>   "Previously released on MS 7031, MS 6533, MS 6743." --
> Container.
>   Programme notes on container.
>   Contents: William Tell -- The voyage to Rheims --
> The thieving magpie -- The Italian woman in Algiers --
> Semiramide -- The silken ladder -- The barber of Seville --
> The Turk in Italy.
>   Columbia records: MG35187.
>
> I. Bernstein, Leonard. II. Szell, George. III.
> New York Philharmonic. IV. Cleveland Orchestra.
> V. Title.

Pre-AACR 2

> Rossini, Gioacchino Antonio, 1792-1868.
>   [Overtures. Selections] [Sound recording]
>   The Rossini overture album. Columbia MG35187
> [1978]
>   2 discs. 33 1/3 rpm. stereo. 12 in. (Colum-
> bia masterworks)
>   New York Philharmonic; Leonard Bernstein, conductor,
> and Cleveland Orchestra, George Szell, conductor.
>   Durations on labels.
>   "Previously released on MS 7031, MS 6533, MS 6743."
>   In container.
>   Program notes on container.
>   Contents: William Tell. -- The voyage to Rheims.
> -- The thieving magpie. -- The Italian woman in
> Algiers. -- Semiramide. -- The silken ladder. -- The
> barber of Seville. -- The Turk in Italy.
>
> I. Bernstein, Leonard, 1917- . II. Szell, George
> Andreas, 1847-1970. III. Philharmonic Society of
> New York. IV. Cleveland Orchestra. V. Title.

(not LC copy; AACR 1, Chapter 14, revised 1976)

<u>Discussion</u>

Description:

   Chief sources of information. The chief sources of information for the description of the AACR 2 record are the labels on the discs. The publisher's number, as well as the numbers applying to the set, appears on each of the four labels (Rule 6.7B19).

Title and statement of responsibility area. Only the title proper and the GMD are recorded in this area. The statement of responsibility is part of the title proper and does not have to be transcribed separately (Rule 1.1B2). It is perhaps important to restate one of the basic principles of AACR 2: Chapter 1 rules apply unless they are superseded by a rule applicable only to a specific format; this is not so in this example. The GMD follows the title proper. The "generic medium designator" in the pre-AACR 2 example is in the uniform title area and does not follow the title proper, as in AACR 2. The position of the GMD under AACR 1 rules depends on the presence of a uniform title; under Chapter 14, revised, the GMD followed the uniform title.

Publication, distribution, etc. area. Each format follows its rules and displays the data in those areas as prescribed. Thus in the AACR 2 example the publisher's number is the last note, but in the pre-AACR 2 example the number is part of the publisher's area.

Physical description area. This AACR 2 example displays the duration in parentheses; only the full minutes and not the seconds are given when the time required to play the disc exceeds five minutes (Rule 6.5B3). The AACR 1 record displays this information in a note. In this instance we chose to indicate that the playing time was given on the labels since this is permitted by the revised Chapter 14.

Note area. We will only briefly discuss here those notes which contain changes or are omitted from the example. AACR 2 does not require to give an "In container" note (Rule 6.7B10). Other physical details are given only when they are of importance. Also note the difference in spelling for "program." We should now use the British "programme" in our notes. This will be one area to which we must pay attention, as we are not in the habit of using this form.

Access points:

Main entry. Rule 21.23B requires entry under the composer since more than one work by the same person has been recorded on the discs.

Added entries. The same rule also prescribes the number of added entries required for the performers. It permits only three added entries for the principal performers, and if there are more than three performers an added entry for only the first one named. The rule is a good one to follow for most libraries; however, it restricts the specialized libraries which may require access to more performers. We decided to break the rules and provide access to the two orchestras since they are among the most prominent in the United States. The same principal was applied for the conductors, Bernstein and Szell. The title added entry was provided according to Rule 21.30J.

Uniform title:

Two rules were applied to formulate the uniform title: 25.36B., for a collection containing the works of one type, and 25.36C, which requires the addition of "Selections" when the first named rule is applied. Rule 25.36B and the word "Overtures" imply that all of a composer's works of the type are included in the uniform title. When that is not the case the word "Selections" must be added (Rule 25.36N). The pre-AACR 2 uniform title is identical, with the exception of the GMD which follows in its own square brackets. The AACR 1 formulation of the uniform title is covered by Rule 239.

Example SR3 (Sound Recording): Two Works / Same Composer

Wagner, Richard
    [Liebesmahl der Apostel]
    Boulez conducts Wagner [sound recording]. --
New York : CBS, 1978.
    1 sound disc. (43 min.) : 33 1/3 rpm, stereo. ;
12 in. -- (Columbia masterworks)
    1st work sung in German.
    New York Philharmonic ; Westminster Choir, Joseph
Flummerfelt, director.
    Programme notes by Edward Downes on container.
    Contents: Love-feast of the apostles -- Siegfried
idyll : original chamber version.
    Columbia : M 35131.

I. Wagner, Richard. Siegfried Idyll. II. Boulez,
Pierre. III. New York Philharmonic. IV. Westminster
Choir. V. Title.

Pre-AACR 2

Wagner, Richard, 1813-1883.
    [Liebesmahl der Apostel. German] [Sound recording]
    Boulez conducts Wagner. Columbia M 35131. [1978]
    1 disc. 33 1/3 rpm. stereo. 12 in. (Columbia
masterworks)
    New York Philharmonic; Westminster Choir, Joseph
Flummerfelt, director.
    1st work sung in German.
    Duration: 43 min., 9 sec.
    Program notes by Edward Downes on container.
    In container.
    Contents: Love-feast of the apostles. -- Siegfried
idyll (original chamber version).

I. Wagner, Richard, 1813-1883. Siegfried Idyll
[Sound recording]. II. Boulez, Pierre, 1925-   .
III. Philharmonic-Symphony Society of New York.
IV. Westminster Choir. V. Title.

(not LC copy)

Discussion

Description:

Chief sources of information. The chief sources of information for a disc under AACR 2 are the labels attached to the disc; these are used to catalog this title. Data not supplied by this source came from the other prescribed sources so interpolation for information from an outside source was not necessary. The revised Chapter 14, AACR 1, also gives the label as one of the areas which supplies the title proper; therefore the bibliographic records are alike.

Title and statement of responsibility area. The title is transcribed as it appears on the label; the titles for the individual works are given in a contents note. Chapter 1 of AACR 2 does not explicitly address the issue of the title transcription for discs with a collective title. Only Rule 2.1B2 (monographs) deals with the condition of a collective title plus titles for the individual works. We decided to follow the pattern set for monographs in this instance since the various rules applied for uniform title made it a viable solution. (We were unable to identify a rule which prohibits this treatment for discs or music.) The composer's name forms part of the title proper and is not repeated (Rules 1.1B2 and 1.1F2). The cataloging for the AACR 1 example is nearly identical since the same source for the description was chosen. In the AACR 1 example, however, the GMD is given with the uniform title, as the rules require; in AACR 2 the GMD always follows the title proper.

Publication, distribution, etc. area. The publication data are taken from the container, since the container is one of the prescribed sources of information (Rule 6.0B2). The publisher's number is the last note in AACR 2 and is not part of this area. The area's sequence of elements does not differ from that for other bibliographic formats, as it does with AACR 1.

Note area. The area follows the order of the elements of the description and gives information on the nature or scope, and the language of the piece. The latter is given when the language of the text cannot be discerned from the description, as is the case here. Thus, the note indicates that the first work is sung in German. The performing groups follow in the next note. Only the choir director's name is given since the conductor's name is implied in the title proper. The contents note differs only in form from the AACR 2 example; the information about the version of the *Siegfried Idyll* is given as other title information and the parentheses have been dropped. Some of the data differ only as to their location in the notes.

Access points:

Main entry. The rule governing the main entry for sound recordings is 21.23B and requires that we "enter a sound recording of two or more works by the same person . . . under the heading appropriate to those works." In this example it is Wagner, the composer of the two pieces performed, and the uniform title of the first piece (see also Rule 25.7).

Added entries. Rule 21.23B also requires access to the performer, the orchestra and the choir. Since the conductor is also a performer, an added entry was also provided for his name. A title added entry was made for the collective title. Rule 21.30J requires a title added entry for works entered under a personal name.

Uniform title:

According to Rule 25.27A, the language of the uniform title is that of the original language. Since we have two works by the same composer published together, we have one work as part of the main entry and the other becomes an author/title added entry (see Rule 25.33). Two works published together also requires us to follow the instructions under 25.7, which obliges us to make a composer/uniform title added entry for the second work, as does Rule 25.33. Note that the language qualifier added to the pre-AACR 2 example is not used for the AACR 2 uniform title. AACR 2 Rules 25.11 and 25.31B7 require a language qualifier only for a translation.

Example SR4 (Sound Recording): Single Work

> Tchaikovsky, Peter Ilich, 1840-1893.
>   Iolanta [sound recording] : opera in one act /
> Tchaikovsky ; libretto M. Tchaikovsky after H.
> Hertz. -- New York : Columbia ; [U.S.S.R.] : Melodiya,
> c1978.
>   2 discs. (90 min.) : 33 1/3 rpm, stereo. ; 12 in.
> --   (Columbia masterworks)
>   Sung in Russian.
>   Tamara Sorokina, Yevgeny Nesterenko, Vladimir
> Atlantov, Yuri Mazurok, Vladimir Valaitis, Alexander
> Arkhipov ; Bolshoi Theater Orchestra and Chorus,
> Mark Ermler, conductor.
>   Recorded in 1976 by Melodiya.
>   Accompanied by translation and transliteration
> of the libretto by Dr. Evangeline Vassiliades and
> programme notes by Boris Schwarz (16 p.).
>   Columbia: M2 34595.
>
>   I. Sorokina, Tamara. II. Nesterenko, Evgenii.
> III. Atlantov, Vladimir. IV. Mazurok, Yuri.
> V. Valaitis, Vladimir. VI. Arkhipov, Alexander.
> VII. Gosudarstvennyi akademicheskii Bolshoi teatr. Orkestr.
> VIII. Ermler, Mark. IX. Title.

Pre-AACR 2

> Chaikovskii, Petr Il'ich, 1840-1893.
>   [Iolanta. Russian] [Sound recording]
>   Iolanta; opera in one act. Libretto by
> M. Tchaikovsky after H. Hertz. Columbia/
> Melodiya M2 34595. [1978] p1976.
>   2 discs. 33 1/3 rpm. Stereo. 12 in.
> (Columbia masterworks)

Sung in Russian.
Tamara Sorokina, Yevgeny Nesterenko, Vladimir Atlantov, Yuri Mazurok, Vladimir Valaitis, Alexander Arkhipov; Bolshoi Theater Orchestra & Chorus, Mark Ermler, conductor.
Recorded in 1976 by Melodiya.
Duration: 90 min., 28 sec.
In container.
Program notes by Boris Schwarz and translation and transliteration of libretto by Dr. Evangeline Vassiliades laid in.

I. Sorokina, Tamara. II. Nesterenko, Evgenii. III. Atlantov, Vladimir. IV. Mazurok, Yuri. V. Valaitis, Vladimir. VI. Arkhipov, Alexander. VII. Ermler, Mark. VIII. Moscow. Gosudarstvennyi akademicheskii Bolshoi teatr. Orkestr. IX. Title.

(LC copy)

Discussion

Description:

Chief sources of information. The chief source of information is the discs' labels, as required by AACR 2, 6.0B1. Chapter 14 of AACR 1 also prefers the label for the transcription of the title; thus the descriptive information of the title, etc. area for the two examples is nearly identical.

Title and statement of responsibility area. In the AACR 2 example the composer follows the other title information found on the disc label. His name is transposed to the required position in the area. In AACR 2 the composer, like the author, does not have to be transcribed when he is the main entry.

Publication, distribution, etc. area. As in the description of other formats the same elements are now also required for sound recordings; this was not the case under earlier rules. The foreign publisher, Melodiya, was also transcribed; however, since only the country could be ascertained its brief form [U.S.S.R.] was given instead of the place name. In the pre-AACR 2 example the two publishers are given but are separated by a slash (/), since both appear on the major source of information.

Note area. After the statement giving the language, the performers were enumerated; this information follows the pattern set by the chief source of information. Since the performers' names are transcribed from the label for both the AACR 2 and the pre-AACR 2 examples, their sequence and form is identical. The date of the initial recording was given in a separate note. The accompanying material note differs; for the AACR 2 example we followed the pattern set for accompanying material by Rule 1.7B11 (the more complex example under 13.6 was not followed). We also, for contrast, kept the phrase "laid in" for the note in the pre-AACR 2 example.

Other notes are in different positions depending on the rules used. AACR 2 requires that the notes follow the pattern of the areas of description and each of the notes can be so identified. Only the first, language of the text, is an exception; it is always first.

"In container," as in the pre-AACR 2 record, should no longer be used. It is redundant according to Rule 6.7B10, since all discs come in a container. Only nonstandard physical details should be given in a note.

Access points:

Main entry. The author of the work, the composer, is the main entry under either code. (For AACR 2 see Rule 21.23A.)

Added entries. Rule 21.23A also requires that only one added entry be made when there are more than three performers named and then only for the first named. This precise rule is very difficult to follow when we are used to making numerous added entries. If one entry must be chosen for this example, it should be the Bolshoi Theater and Orchestra, not the soprano, who is the first performer named in the example. We followed our old practices, although we tried to stay as close as possible to the AACR 2 rules.

Uniform title:

We decided not to add a uniform title since the title proper and the uniform title would be identical. AACR 2 states that a uniform title "provide[s] the means for bringing together all catalogue entries for a work . . . [if it has] appeared under various titles." There is no variant title in this case.

MICROFORMS

The concepts for cataloging microforms have been completely reversed in AACR 2. The new concepts require that we describe the form of the publication in hand and not its original manifestation. AACR 2 adopts this principle from ISBD(NBM) (nonbook materials), which includes microforms. Like ISBD(NBM), the introductory statement in AACR 2 Rule 0.24, "Methods of Procedure," requires that we consult the guidelines for the item's original format. The five examples we show for this format illustrate some of the changes. (One of the examples, S3, is a serial and is presented in the section on serials.)

Title and Statement of Responsibility

The rules for selecting the chief source of information specify the original title page instead of the title frame of the microform (Rule 11.0B1). Depending on the type of microform, eye-readable data and the container may serve as that source, but these follow a specific order of preference given by the rule. When only the original's chief source of information is available, the data are transcribed from it; however, they are enclosed in square brackets as data from outside the chief source of information (compare Examples MF1 and MF2).

Chapter 11 (Microforms) is new to the code, so few comparisons can be drawn. Like all other chapters, it relies heavily on Chapter 1 and includes references to the chapters which treat the original form of the item. Area three, the numeric and/or chronological designations area, which applies only to maps and serials at this time, refers to the specific rules in Chapters 3 and 12, respectively. The rules for the original of the microform copy apply in this area.

Publication, Distribution, etc.

The imprint follows the form established in Chapter 1, and the options stated there can also be applied to microforms, if the decision has been made to apply them. If there is no place of publication or publisher the "s.n." and/or "s.l." provisions must be employed. A date is always provided, even if it is only an estimate (see Rule 1.4F), as in Example MF1.

Physical Description

Specific material designations are also supplied in the physical description area. The number of items constituting the whole are given even if it is only one piece—e.g., "1 microfilm reel." Microfilms are also described in terms of their container, i.e., cassette, cartridge or reel, but if the GMD is applied the prefix "micro" may be dropped (compare Examples MF1 and MF2). Accompanying material is recorded in the same manner as for other formats.

Series Area

In the series area the microform series is transcribed. The original series is given in a note, as is also done with bound reprints (see Rules 1.7B12 and 1.11F).

Notes

The notes have their specified order. First all notes relating to the microform are presented; the details relating to the original are combined into one note. The data describing the original follow the order of the areas of description and their elements. We must assume that the note describing the original is the last note and would be followed by the ISBN or ISSN assigned to the microform.

The standard number and terms of availability rules are included in Chapter 11, and will apply when ISBNs or ISSNs, or an equivalent, are also identifying microforms.

EXAMPLE MF1

Title Frame of Microfilm

DOCTORAL DISSERTATION SERIES

TITLE *THE RISE, DEVELOPMENT, DECLINE AND INFLUENCE OF THE AMERICAN MINSTREL SHOW*

AUTHOR *FRANK COSTELLOW*

UNIVERSITY *NEW YORK UNIV.* DATE *1952*

DEGREE *Ph.D.* PUBLICATION NO. *4515*

UNIVERSITY MICROFILMS
ANN ARBOR • MICHIGAN

Title Page of Original on Microfilm

Sponsoring Committee: Professor Fred Blanchard
Associate Professor: Harry G. Cayley, and
Associate Professor: Durward Pruden

THE RISE, DEVELOPMENT, DECLINE AND INFLUENCE
OF THE AMERICAN MINSTREL SHOW

FRANK COSTELLOW DAVIDSON

Submitted in partial fulfillment of the
requirements of the Degree of Doctor of
Philosophy in the School of Education of
New York University

1952

EXAMPLE MF2

First Frame—Copy of Microfilming Request

49825

ORDER FOR PHOTODUPLICATION TO

THE LIBRARY OF CONGRESS
PHOTODUPLICATION SERVICE

WASHINGTON, D. C. 20540

MICROFILM (0/63)

MAKE CHECK OR MONEY ORDER PAYABLE TO
CHIEF, PHOTODUPLICATION SERVICE, LIBRARY OF CONGRESS

F-4

University of Nebraska Libraries
Acquisition Department
Lincoln, Nebraska

Signature

Date of Request

Customer's Order No.

PS

Deposit Account No.

Mail ☑ Pick Up ☐

Type of reproduction (see reverse):
☐ Electrostatic Positive Prints (Xerox) ☐ Photostat ☑ Microfilm ☐ Photograph ☐

☑ Negative ☐ Positive

Exp. @ $

LECTURES

ON THE

SACRED POETRY

OF THE

HEBREWS.

TRANSLATED FROM THE LATIN OF THE LATE

RIGHT REV. ROBERT LOWTH, D. D.
PRELECTOR OF POETRY IN THE UNIVERSITY OF OXFORD,
AND LORD BISHOP OF LONDON,

BY G. GREGORY, F. A. S.
Author of Essays Historical and Moral.

TO WHICH ARE ADDED,
THE PRINCIPAL NOTES OF PROFESSOR MICHAELIS,
AND
NOTES BY THE TRANSLATOR AND OTHERS.

THE SECOND EDITION.

IN TWO VOLUMES.
VOL. II.

LONDON:
PRINTED FOR OGLES, DUNCAN, AND COCHRAN,
37, PATERNOSTER ROW, AND 295, HOLBORN;
J. OGLE, Parliament Square, Edinburgh; and M. OGLE, Glasgow.
1816.

Title Page of Volume 2

LECTURES

ON THE

SACRED POETRY

OF THE

HEBREWS.

TRANSLATED FROM THE LATIN OF THE LATE

RIGHT REV. ROBERT LOWTH, D. D.
PRELECTOR OF POETRY IN THE UNIVERSITY OF OXFORD,
AND LORD BISHOP OF LONDON,

BY G. GREGORY, F. A. S.
Author of Essays Historical and Moral.

TO WHICH ARE ADDED,
THE PRINCIPAL NOTES OF PROFESSOR MICHAELIS,
AND
NOTES BY THE TRANSLATOR AND OTHERS.

THE SECOND EDITION.

IN TWO VOLUMES.
VOL. I.

LONDON:
PRINTED FOR OGLES, DUNCAN, AND COCHRAN,
37, PATERNOSTER ROW, AND 295, HOLBORN;
J. OGLE, Parliament Square, Edinburgh; and M. OGLE, Glasgow.
1816.

Title Page of Volume 1

EXAMPLE: MF3

CONDILLAC E.B. de – Principes gé- néraux de grammaire pour toutes langues. Paris, 1798.	ⓒ MICROEDITIONS HACHETTE
	71 5038

Eye-Readable Data from Top of Microfiche

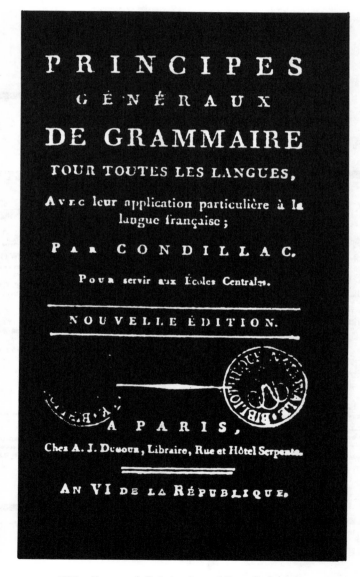

Title Page of Original on Microfiche

**Title Page of Original
on Microfiche**

ELECTRICAL NOISE

*Fundamentals and
Physical Mechanism*

D. A. BELL, M.A., Ph.D., M.I.E.E.

*Reader in Electromagnetism
University of Birmingham*

D. VAN NOSTRAND COMPANY, LTD

LONDON

TORONTO **NEW YORK**

PRINCETON, NEW JERSEY

D. VAN NOSTRAND COMPANY, LTD.
358, Kensington High Street, London, W.14, England

D. VAN NOSTRAND COMPANY (Canada), LTD.
25 Hollinger Road, Toronto 16, Canada

D. VAN NOSTRAND COMPANY, INC.
120 Alexander St., Princeton, New Jersey
257 Fourth Avenue, New York 10, New York

———————

Library of Congress Catalog Card No. 59-11055

Verso of Title Page on Microfiche

Example MF1 (Microfilm Manuscript): Microform Publisher

> Davidson, Frank Costellow.
>   The rise, development, decline and influence of
> the American minstrel show [microform] / Frank
> Costellow Davidson. -- Ann Arbor, Mich. : University
> Microfilms, [197-?].
>   1 microfilm reel : ill., facsims., music ; 35 mm.
>   Thesis (Ph.D.) -- New York University, 1952.
>   Bibliographies: leaves 13-16, 216-230.
>   Originally submitted: 1952. 1-16, iv, 254 leaves.
>
>   I. Title.

Pre-AACR 2

> Davidson, Frank Costellow, 1908--
>   The rise, development, decline and influence of
> the American minstrel show / Frank Costellow
> Davidson. -- 1952.
>   16, iv, 254 leaves : ill., facsims., music.
>   Bibliographies: leaves 13-16, 216-230.
>   Thesis--New York University.
>   Microfilm typescript. Ann Arbor, Mich. : Univer-
> sity Microfilms, 1980?. -- 1 reel ; 35 mm.
>
>   I. Title.

(not LC copy; AACR 1, Chapter 6, revised)

Discussion

Description:

Chief sources of information. The chief source of information is the title frame; it includes the full bibliographic data necessary to describe the item, except the date. Rule 0.24 requires that the item be cataloged according to the "class" of material to which it belongs, and Rule 11.0B1, "Chief source of information," gives the title frame that status.

Title and statement of responsibility area. The records are nearly alike in this area; only the GMD was added. The GMD is the generic term "microform"; it is applied to all microform formats (Rule 1.1C1).

Publication, distribution, etc. area. This area reflects the new thinking which determines the contents of a bibliographic record for microforms. Rule 0.24 states clearly that ". . . the starting point for description is the physical form for the item in hand." Consequently the publishing information in the AACR 2 record reflects this fact and gives University Microfilms as the publisher. The date of microfilming is uncertain; only the decade could be assumed. Therefore, applying Rule 1.4F7, the date is given as "[197-?]."
Remember that a thesis is a manuscript and not a published monograph; this definition

was already applied under AACR 1, and the imprint area of the pre-AACR 2 record reflects this treatment; only the date of acceptance of the thesis appears in this area.

Physical description area. The physical description also reflects Rule 0.24 and only the microfilm information is given. Rule 11.5B1 specifies the terms describing microforms; for this example the term is "microfilm." The rule recommends that the prefix "micro" be dropped when the GMD is used in the first area (title and statement of responsibility). Since this is also a local policy decision, the specific material designation "microfilm" is used in this example, but not in the later ones. The area's contents, therefore, describe the film and not the original item; that information is recorded in the note relating to the original. Here we enumerate the number of reels, illustration information and the dimension, the latter in "mm."

Note area. In this area all notes relating to the microfilm publication are given first, followed by the note relating to the original. All information about the original is to be recorded in one note, and the details are given in the order in which they relate to the areas and their elements of description. As stated above, a thesis is a manuscript. Thus the information about the original contains only the date; there is no information on publisher, etc. Then follows the physical description of the original. Only the dimensions could not be established. Note that with AACR 2 the term "thesis" is followed by the abbreviation designating the degree for the Ph.D.; under the previous rules only the fact that a thesis was not produced for the Ph.D. degree was given.

Access points:

Main entry. Rule 21.1A2 requires entry under the personal name when the work can be attributed to an individual.

Added entries. An added entry is provided for the title when the main entry is a personal name (Rule 21.30J).

Example MF2 (Microfilm Monograph): Library as Manufacturer of Copy

> Lowth, Robert, 1710-1787.
>   [De sacra poesi Hebraeorum. English]
>   [Lectures on the sacred poetry of the Hebrews [microform] / translated from the Latin of Robert Lowth by G. Gregory ; to which are added the principal notes of Professor Michaelis and notes by the translator and others]. -- Washington : Library of Congress, Photoduplication Service, 1966.
>   1 film reel : negative, ports. ; 35 mm.
>   Includes bibliographical references and index.
>   Originally issued as: 2nd ed. London : printed for Ogles, Duncan, and Cochran, 1816. 2 v.
>
>   I. Title.

Pre-AACR 2

> Lowth, Robert, Bp. of London, 1710-1787.
> [De sacra poesi Hebraeorum. English]
> Lectures on the sacred poetry of the Hebrews translated from the Latin of Robert Lowth by G. Gregory ; to which are added the principal notes of Professor Michaelis and notes by the translator and others. -- 2n ed. -- London : printed for Ogles, Duncan, and Cochran, 1816.
> 2 v. : port. ; 21 cm.
> Includes bibliographical references and index.
> Microform (negative). Washington : Library of Congress, Photoduplication Service, 1966. -- 1 reel ; 36 mm.
>
> I. Title.

(not LC copy)

Discussion

Description:

Chief sources of information. The chief source of information is the title frame; it is lacking on this film. As a result all descriptive data is given in brackets. The initial frame of the film is the microfilmed order request. It gives the copying date, which is transcribed as the last element of the publication, etc. area.

Title and statement of responsibility area. All data were taken from the title page copy of the original. Since this is not the chief source of information, the data must be placed in square brackets as required by Rule 11.0B2.

Edition area. Note that the edition statement given on the original title page is not transcribed in this area. It is given in a note. The edition statement applies only to the original; the microfilm copy lacks an edition statement as it does the title page information. Rule 11.2B1, the rule for the edition statement for microforms, refers us to 1.2B, the general rule applying to this area. Under 1.2B4 we have the option to add an edition statement when we know that the item contains additional information. The option was not taken. It is not advisable to assign an edition statement on the assumption that the copy in hand is a later edition, i.e., not the first. Also note the change in the ordinal numbers. In AACR 1 the ordinal number is "2d" (AACR 1, p. 368), in AACR 2 it is "2nd" (AACR 2, p. 562).

Publication, distribution, etc. area. In this example the microfilming agency, Library of Congress, is recorded. Its name is given on the last frame of the film and on the first frame of the filmed photocopy request form. The information is transcribed without brackets since it was taken from one of the prescribed sources of information, "the rest of the item" (Rule 11.0B2). We gave the status of "rest of the item" to these two frames because they are a physical part of the film.

Physical description area. To exemplify the option of dropping the qualifier "micro" from the basic term "film," we described the item as in the example above; thus the physical description contains only "film reel." However, the item is a negative copy of the original and this fact should be given according to Rule 11.5C1. Although the rule does not specifically state that the "negative" precedes other data recorded as part of this element, the fact that the rule is in the first position is sufficient to make this assumption. The last example under Rule 11.5C2 verifies this conclusion.

Note area. The second note contains the information about the original. Rule 11.7B2 requires that the details be combined and given ". . . in the order of the area to which they relate."

Access points:

Main entry. Rule 21.1A2, the general rule for entry under personal name, applies here. Lowth is the principal author; therefore, the entry is his name, an easy decision.

Added entries. A title entry is obvious and required by Rule 21.30J. Rule 21.30K1 also requires an added entry for the translator but only under certain conditions. None of the conditions apply to this example and an added entry is not made. A brief comparison with AACR 1's provisions for an added entry under the translator, Rule 33E, indicates that the rule has been expanded, but there is no change in those provisions which required an added entry for the translator.

Example MF3 (Microfiche Monograph): Microform Publisher & Edition

> Condillac, Étienne Bonnot de, 1714-1780.
>   Principes généraux de grammaire pour toutes langues [microform] / E.B. de Condillac. -- Micro-editions. -- [Paris] : Hachette, [1971].
>   7 microfiches : 11 x 15 cm.
>   "71-5038."
>   Originally published as: Principes généraux de grammaire pour toutes les langues : avec leur application particulière à la langue française / par Condillac. Nouv. ed. Paris : A.J. Dugour, An VI de la République [1798]. 398 p.
>
>   I. Title.

Pre-AACR 2

> Condillac, Étienne Bonnot de, 1714-1780.
>   Principes généraux de grammaire pour toutes langues : avec leur application particulière à la langue française / par Condillac. -- Nouv. ed. -- Paris : A.J. Dugour, An VI de la République [1798].
>   398 p.

(cont'd.)

> Microfiche. Paris : Hachette, 1971. 7 sheets :
> 11 x 15 cm.
> "71-5038."
>
> I. Title.

(not LC copy; AACR 1, Chapter 6, revised)

Discussion

Description:

Chief sources of information. The item does not contain a title frame, the preferred choice as chief source of information; however, it does have "eye-readable" data which may substitute for the title frame as chief source of information.

Title and statement of responsibility area. This information is transcribed in the order of the elements as required by Rule 1.1F3 and not as it appears on the eye-readable information on the fiches. We also changed the order of the personal name so that it follows the normal sequence. The title proper differs from the original, which is given below in the note area.

Edition area. The fiche also contains a microform edition statement; at least the statement appearing above the publisher's name was interpreted as such.

Publication, distribution, etc. area. The microform publisher's name is transcribed from the fiche; the other required information is interpolated from outside sources and placed in square brackets. Each element has its own set of brackets in this example since an element not requiring brackets intervenes.

Physical description area. Microfiche is described only as such; no additional descriptor is necessary. AACR 2 has one qualifier for microfiche, the term "cassette," but it does not apply here. The term "sheet" employed in AACR 1 is no longer applicable. The number of fiches is followed by the physical details, when they are applicable. These include the word "negative" for a copy in this form. The size is the last element and as in AACR 1 it is given in "cm."

Note area. The first note is the number transcribed from the fiche; it applies only to the microform. The second note relates to the original. The full title proper and other title information are transcribed; the publication data are provided. The date is not in the conventional form, but is recorded as it appears and followed by the year in the Gregorian or Julian calendar (Rule 1.4F1). The physical description consists only of the extent of the original; the original size was not established.

Access points:

Main entry. As with all previous rules, the name of a personal author becomes the main entry, and AACR 2 does not break with this convention (Rule 21.1A2). The full and established form is used. Only the last name appears in the original, but the initials and name appear on the fiche.

Added entries. When a personal name is the main entry the title nearly always is an added access point (Rule 21.30J). An added entry for the title including the dropped word "les" was not provided since "les" appears before the last word in the title and its absense is not likely to cause retrieval problems. No other added entries are required.

Example MF4 (Microfiche Monograph): Without Microform Publisher or Manufacturer

> Bell, D.A. (David Arthur)
>   Electrical noise [microform] / A.D. Bell. --
> [S.1. : s.n., 196-?].
>   4 microfiches : ill. ; 11 x 15 cm.
>   Includes bibliographical references and index.
>   Originally issued: Electrical noise : fundamentals
> and physical mechanism. London ; New York :
> Van Nostrand, 1960. x, 342 p. ; 24 cm.
>
>   I. Title.

Pre-AACR 2

> Bell, David Arthur.
>   Electrical noise : fundamentals and physical
> mechanism / D. A. Bell. -- London ; New York :
> Van Nostrand, 1960.
>   x, 342 p. : ill. ; 24 cm.
>   Includes bibliographical references and
> index.
>   Microfiche. 4 sheets ; 11 x 15 cm.
>
>   I. Title.

(not LC copy; AACR 1, Chapter 6, revised)

Discussion

Description:

Chief sources of information. The eye-readable data on the top of the fiche serve as the chief source of information since the first choice, the title frame, is not available (Rule 11.0B1).

Title and statement of responsibility area. The title proper is transcribed as it appears on the fiche and is followed by the GMD. Other title information is not available on the chief source of information. The personal author's name is the third and last element of the area.

Publication, distribution, etc. area. Publication data are not present and also not available from another source. AACR 2 requires that the lack of this information be indicated by employing the abbreviations for the Latin "sine loco" (without place) and "sine nomine" (without name) — "S.l." and "s.n." (Rules 1.4C6 and 1.4D6). Date of publication information must also be supplied (Rule 1.4F7); we can at least estimate the decade as being the 1960s. The area is surrounded with brackets because all elements are supplied (Rule 1.0C, paragraph 6). Since the rules quoted here are part of Chapter 1, they apply to any format; Chapter 11, Rule 11.4B, refers to these rules specifically.

Physical description area. In this area the fiches are enumerated and their size is stated. When the item contains illustrative material, it is also given here. The order of the elements is fixed and cannot be changed; the extent of the item (i.e., the number of fiches) is followed by other physical detail and then by the size.

Note area. The first note relates to the microform and indicates the presence of a bibliography and an index. It is followed by the description of the original. The title proper and the other title information are transcribed, since the former is so general that more detailed identification appeared desirable to differentiate this title from another in the catalog. The author's name is identical with the first statement of responsibility and is not transcribed a second time. The publication data follow, with the physical description for the original, since it could be established without effort.

The description of the microfiche employing the pre-AACR 2 rules gives opposite results. That is, the original is described first and the microfiche data appear in the note area. Under these rules the publication data for the microform were given only when they were readily available (AACR 1, Chapter 6, revised, Rule 156.B2).

Access points:

Main entry. Rule 21.1A2 determines that the main entry for a work by a personal author is that of the author's name.

Added entries. An added title entry must be provided for an item when it is entered under a personal name (Rule 21.30J), at least most of the time. (For details see the cited rule.)

SERIALS

Serials present extraordinary problems for the cataloger. There are identical and/or generic titles, changing titles, changing frequencies, merging titles and titles that separate. After AACR 1 was published in 1967 librarians began to slowly adopt the cataloging changes. They stopped changing a serial record to the new form of the title; instead, complying with the rules, they began to make new records for each successive title. Then it was recognized that library users really approached periodicals under their initials or acronyms: JAMA, for example. Most librarians may also pause for a moment to recollect the name the initials represent (Journal of the American Medical Association). Periodical serials were then entered under their initialisms. Generic titles, such as Bulletin, Journal or Report, had to be differentiated from one another for filing and retrieval. They were made "distinctive" by adding the author to the title and preceding the latter with a space-hyphen-space (-).

The idea of the generic title has not been continued in AACR 2. "Unique titles" may have to be formulated in order to deal with identical titles in serials and series, as previously mentioned in this chapter. At this time, we must wait for the results of the requested rule amendment and publication. The unique title includes the concept of the key title. This is a title assigned to and so uniquely identifying one serial; an ISSN and its key title are inseparable. Patterns of the past repeat; cataloging rules for serials continue to change, even before anyone has tested them.

The examples presented for serials were selected to illustrate the difficulties this format presents. We also included a personal author serial (Example S9) and a monographic publisher's series cataloged as a serial (Example S10); its companion monographic record is Example M18. As with the other formats, the GMD (general material designation) is provided for all examples.

The first rule change encountered is the choice of issue—which volume the cataloging data is to be taken from. In AACR 2, it is the first issue or volume received. In AACR 1, it was the latest issue available. The establishment of chief and prescribed sources of information will increase similarity in bibliographic records and enhance their interchangeability.

Title and Statement of Responsibility

The general rules predominate in the transcription of the title proper. However, these rules are amplified to accommodate a variety of idiosyncracies of serial publications (Rules 12.1B3-5). Rule 12.1B6 changes the treatment of ordinal or cardinal numbers in a serial title. Formerly the numeric was omitted (AACR 1 Rule 162C); the new rules require the omission mark (...) unless the number precedes the title, in which case it is dropped (see Example S8).

Parallel titles are also treated like monographs (Example S6) but a special provision has been given to parallel titles with a parallel section title. Other title information is transcribed as required by Rule 1.1E and not relegated to the note area as under AACR 1 unless necessary for the identification of the title proper. Example S1 illustrates Rule 12.1E1; it also presents an initialism as the title proper.

We will find that the statement of responsibility accompanies a title more often (see Example S8), since the restrictions on its transcription have been largely eliminated. However, we continue to list editors and personal publishers in the notes area (Rule 12.1F3).

The rules dealing with editions in Rule 1.2B also apply to serials. Special note must be taken of the limitations and specifications which apply only to serials (see Rules 12.2B1-B4).

Numeric/Alphabetic, etc. Designation

The numeric and/or alphabetic, chronological or other designation area contains new punctuation and a clarification for the treatment of multilanguage chronological designations. These rules will probably be easier to apply since they are more systematically laid out. Librarians who only occasionally catalog a serial should be able to get along quite efficiently with these rules.

Publication, Distribution, etc.

The publication, distribution, etc. area follows that of Chapter 1. The date of publication of the first volume or issue is given, even when it is the same as the chronological designation for the first volume in the chronological area of the record. The publication date is *not* omitted from the AACR 2 record.

Physical Description

The extent of item rules are those of the format or type of material to which the serial belongs. For sound recordings Rule 6.5B applies; microforms are described by applying Rule 11.5B, etc. This also holds true for other physical details and the dimensions. Material accompanying a serial is treated according to Rule 1.5E; a note (Rule 12.7B11) indicates its frequency.

Series Area

There is no difference in the series area rule; all of AACR 2 Rule 1.6 applies.

Notes

The notes, in addition to those used in Chapter 1, display the frequency, variations in title and relationship to other serials. The last type is comparable to the edition and history note for the other formats. The difference is that it is largely expanded (compare with AACR 1 Rules 167G-H and Q). Other notes may be added, such as other formats available, audience, accompanying material and notes relating to important numbers other than the ISSN. The latter would include U.N. document numbers, Superintendent of Documents' numbers or local document number, for example. In a shared data base the note indicating the basis of the description, if it is other than the first issue, can aid in avoiding duplication of records because it will explain differences in the data of the records.

The ISSN, key title and terms of availability are now clearly defined. They are the last note in the serial description.

EXAMPLE S1

Cover with Initials and Full Title

Verso of Title Page

The PEABODY JOURNAL OF EDUCATION is interdisciplinary and is designed to foster the professional development and enrichment of teachers, administrators, and other leaders in education. The JOURNAL carries full-length articles and short contributions as well as book reviews, editorial comment, and occasional special features of interest to faculty and administrators alike.

Manuscripts should be addressed to Ralph E. Kirkman, Editor, PEABODY JOURNAL OF EDUCATION, George Peabody College for Teachers, Nashville, Tennessee 37203. Manuscripts should be double spaced on 8½ x 11 bond and should follow "The MLA Style Sheet." An original and two copies should be submitted. Unsolicited contributions should be accompanied by a stamped, self-addressed envelope.

Correspondence concerning subscriptions and single issues should be addressed to the Executive Secretary. Claims for undelivered copies must be made within two months following the month of publication.

The JOURNAL is indexed in *Education Index, Current Index to Journals in Education,* the *Book Review Index,* and *Current Contents, Education.*

The PEABODY JOURNAL OF EDUCATION is published four times a year in October, January, April, and July by George Peabody College for Teachers, Nashville, Tennessee 37203. Volume begins with the October issue. Subscriptions to libraries and organizations, $8.00 a year; private individuals, $6.00 a year; foreign subscriptions, $1.00 extra. Single issues, $1.75.

Second-class postage paid at Nashville, Tennessee.

PEABODY JOURNAL OF EDUCATION

Copyright © 1970 by George Peabody College for Teachers. All rights reserved.

Title Page

EXAMPLE S2

1st Available Issue for Cataloging

ISSN
Subscription Price
From Later Issue

family health

HEALTH POWER
Four Keys to a Longer, Happier Life

1
MEDICINE'S
TARGET:
THE TOP
TEN KILLERS
2
THE QUIZ
THAT COULD
LENGTHEN
YOUR LIFE
3
VEGETABLES:
TOMORROW'S
FOOD
TODAY
4
HELPING
YOUR
DOCTOR
HELP YOU

Microfilm Title Page of
1st Available Reel

CURRENT PERIODICAL SERIES

PUBLICATION NO: 10,761

TITLE: FAMILY HEALTH

VOLUME: 7   ISSUES: 1-12

DATE: January - December 1975

NOTICE: This periodical may be copyrighted, in which case the contents remain
the property of the copyright owner. The microfilm edition is reproduced by agreement with the publisher. Duplication or resale without permission is prohibited.

University Microfilms International, Ann Arbor Mich.

MICROFILMED — 1978

EXAMPLE S4

Cover of Superseded Title

HEAT AND FLUID FLOW

The JOURNAL of the Thermodynamics and Fluid Mechanics Group of the Institution of Mechanical Engineers

Vol. 8   No. 2   October 1978

IANICS GROUP OF THE

H.C. Simpson (*Vice Chairman*)

Published by MECHANICAL ENGINEERING PUBLICATIONS LTD, London and Birmingham, Alabama for THE INSTITUTION OF MECHANICAL ENGINEERS (Tel: 01-839 1211).

Editorial Office: P.O. Box 24, Northgate Avenue, Bury St. Edmunds, Suffolk IP32 6BW (Tel: 0284 63277).

Price: Annual Subscription Rates, two issues: Members £8.00; Non-members in the United Kingdom and Eire £12.00 Non-members elsewhere £16.00

Contents Page with Publication Information

158

EXAMPLE S5

Cover of 1st Issue Under New Title

The International Journal of

Heat and Fluid Flow

Vol 1 No 1 March 1979

al of

id

and Birmingham, Alabama, in consultation nstitution of Mechanical Engineers.

Contents Page: Publications Data

Publisher's Note Indicating Relationship to Earlier Title

THE INTERNATIONAL JOURNAL OF
HEAT AND FLUID FLOW

By way of introduction . . .

In April 1971 the Thermodynamics and Fluid Mechanics Group of the Institution of Mechanical Engineers introduced the journal *Heat and Fluid Flow* as a clearly identifiable publication within which selected matter of specific concern to the Group could be found.

Since then successive issues have included a number of important papers originally accepted by the Institution for publication in its Proceedings or occasionally in other of its technical journals.

In recent years the Committee of the Thermodynamics and Fluid Mechanics Group has recognized the need for the journal to give greater emphasis to the engineering and experimental aspects of its activities and, through more rapid publication, to improve the service it offers to the practising engineer and designer.

To meet these objectives, the Group Committee has decided that from April 1979 its journal shall become an international quarterly entitled *The International Journal of Heat and Fluid Flow* in which original contributions of more immediate interest to the practising engineer will be published. This is therefore the last issue of the journal in its present form.

Though intended to be complementary to existing publications of the Institution of Mechanical Engineers, the new journal will be independently administered by an Honorary Editorial Advisory Board through its Editors-in-Chief and published by Mechanical Engineering Publications Ltd. The journal will be available for purchase by annual subscription.

Manuscripts (in triplicate) may be submitted to any Consultant Editor or Editor-in-Chief as given hereunder but overseas authors are advised to select the one nearest at hand. The standards for acceptance will be those of the learned societies and the decision of the Editors-in-Chief shall be final. Every effort will be made to ensure rapid publication. The journal will be published in the English language and will include shorter communications, correspondence on papers, and book reviews, together with selected advertising material.

Submissions will be welcomed on the experimental and associated analytical aspects of engineering thermofluid dynamics and heat transfer, including flow measurement, relevant instrumentation developments and data processing, and their application through design and development to the whole field of thermal and fluid power plant and processes, including consideration of energy resources, energy conversion and conservation.

EXAMPLE S6

Verso of Contents

CANADIAN JOURNAL OF
BEHAVIOURAL SCIENCE

REVUE CANADIENNE DES
SCIENCES DU COMPORTEMENT

Editor: ARTHUR M. SULLIVAN

Rédacteur en chef

Assistant Editors: ADRIEN PINARD, DAVID S. HART

Adjoints au rédacteur en chef

Editorial Board:

Comité de Rédaction

A. J. Arrowood, G. A. Auclair, H. D. Beach, S. S. Blank, W. H. Coons, C. C. Costello,
P. C. Dodwell, W. H. Gaddes, D. E. Hunt, J. Inglis, D. N. Jackson, R. E. LaPointe,
R. S. MacArthur, D. R. Olson, E. C. Poser, T. J. Ryan.

THE CANADIAN JOURNAL OF BEHAVIOURAL
SCIENCE is published quarterly. Annual
subscription, $7.50, single number, $2.00
Contributions. Original manuscripts and
correspondence on editorial matters
should be sent to:

LA REVUE CANADIENNE DES SCIENCES DU'
COMPORTEMENT est une revue trimes-
trielle. Prix de l'abonnement annuel:
$7.50; prix du numéro: $2.00
Articles. Adresser comme suit tout
article à publier et toute correspondance

Cover of 1st Issue

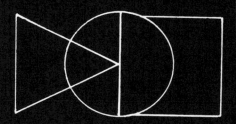

No. 1 JANUARY 1969

Canadian
Journal of
Behavioural
Science

Psychological Association by University of Toronto Press

nadienne de Psychologie par University of Toronto Press

Revue
canadienne
des
sciences du
comportement

No. 1 JANVIER 1969

Title Page of 1st Issue Published Later

Canadian Journal of Behavioural Science

VOLUME 1, 1969

Revue canadienne des Sciences du comportement

Editor/Rédacteur en chef:

ARTHUR M. SULLIVAN, Memorial University of Newfoundland

Assistant Editors/Adjoints au rédacteur en chef:

DAVID S. HART, Memorial University of Newfoundland
ADRIEN PINARD, University of Montreal

Editorial Board/Comité de Rédaction:

A. J. ARROWOOD, *University of Toronto*
G. A. AUCLAIR, *Ecole des Hautes Etudes Commerciales*
H. D. BEACH, *Dalhousie University*
S. S. BLANK, *University of British Columbia*
W. H. COONS, *York University*
C. C. COSTELLO, *University of Calgary*
P. C. DODWELL, *Queen's University*
W. H. GADDES, *University of Victoria*
D. E. HUNT, *Ontario Institute for Studies in Education*
J. INGLIS, *Queen's University*
D. N. JACKSON, *University of Western Ontario*
R. E. LAPOINTE, *University of Montreal*
R. S. MACARTHUR, *University of Alberta*
D. R. OLSON, *Ontario Institute for Studies in Education*
A. PAIVIO, *University of Western Ontario*
E. C. POSER, *McGill University*
T. J. RYAN, *Carleton University*

Published for the Canadian Psychological Association by
PUBLIÉ POUR LA SOCIÉTÉ CANADIENNE DE PSYCHOLOGIE PAR
UNIVERSITY OF TORONTO PRESS

EXAMPLE S7

Cover of 1st Issue

Number 1

January, 1967

PHARMACEUTICAL CHEMISTRY JOURNAL

ХИМИКО-ФАРМАЦЕВТИЧЕСКИЙ ЖУРНАЛ

(KHIMIKO-FARMATSEVTICHESKII ZHURNAL)

TRANSLATED FROM RUSSIAN

 CONSULTANTS BUREAU

s a cover-to-cover translation
rnal, a publication of the Min-

dnaya Kniga, the Soviet book
th advance copies of the Rus-
notographs and artwork. This
time lag between publication
the translation and helps to
The Russian original and the
67 issues.

sevticheskii Zhurnal:

O. Yu. Magidson
M. D. Mashkovskii
N. M. Shmakov
A. P. Skoldinov
E. R. Valashek

Subscription
(12 Issues): $80

(Add $5 for orders outside the United States and Canada.)

Single Issue: $30
Single Article: $15

Order from:

CONSULTANTS BUREAU
227 West 17th Street, New York, New York 10011

Verso of 1st Issue

162

Cover of Later Issue Listing ISSN, CODEN

ISSN 0091-150X

Russian Original Vol. 11, No. 5, Part 1, May, 1977

March 10, 1978

PCJOAU 11(5) 587-656 (1977)

PHARMACEUTICAL CHEMISTRY JOURNAL

Pharmaceutical Chemistry Journal is a cover-to-cover translation of *Khimiko-Farmatsevticheskii Zhurnal*, a publication of the Ministry of Public Health of the USSR.

An agreement with the Copyright Ag[...] makes available both advance copies [...] original glossy photographs and artwo[...] the necessary time lag between publi[...] publication of the translation and he[...] of the latter. The translation began [...] Russian journal.

Editorial Board of *Khimiko-Farmatsevi[...]*

Editor: D. Kh. Skalaban

Associate Editors: P. G. Glushkov and [...]

Secretaries: L. Ya. Dorofeev and A. P[...]

N. A. Afanas'ev	K. Y[...]
A. P. Arzamastsev	M. N[...]
A. I. Brykin	E. A[...]
V. I. Gunar	E. E[...]
S. M. Kagiyants	A. P[...]
V. M. Kantere	R. D[...]
Yu. F. Kolosov	G. V[...]
V. P. Labzin	O. L[...]
M. D. Mashkovskii	E. R[...]
P. P. Neugodov	A. M[...]

Russian Original Vol. 5, No. 1, January, 1971

Translation published August, 1971

PHARMACEUTICAL CHEMISTRY JOURNAL

ХИМИКО-ФАРМАЦЕВТИЧЕСКИЙ ЖУРНАЛ
(KHIMIKO-FARMATSEVTICHESKII ZHURNAL)

TRANSLATED FROM RUSSIAN

$\frac{c}{b}$ CONSULTANTS BUREAU, NEW YORK

Cover of Issue
with New Enumeration

Subscription (24 Issues):
Vol. 13: $335
Vol. 14: $375

Single Issue: $50
Single Article: $7.50

CONSULTANTS BUREAU, NEW YORK AND LONDON

$\frac{c}{b}$ 227 West 17th Street
New York, New York 10011

Published semimonthly, consisting of Volume 13 issues 3 Part 1 through 12 Part 2 and Volume 14 issues 1 Part 1 through 2 Part 2. Subscription price for Volume 13 is $335, and for Volume 14 is $375. Second-class postage paid at Jamaica, New York 11431.

Verso of Cover of Latest Issue Listing Price

Title Page of 2nd Issue

NATIONAL ADVISORY COUNCIL

ON ECONOMIC OPPORTUNITY

National Advisory Council on Economic Opportunity

TENTH REPORT MARCH 1978

NINTH REPORT

MARCH 31, 1977

For sale by the Superintendent of Documents, U.S. Government Printing Office
Washington, D.C. 20402
Stock Number 041-008-00016-4

Cover of 1st Issue Under New Title

NATIONAL ADVISORY COUNCIL
ON ECONOMIC OPPORTUNITY
1725 K STREET, N.W., SUITE 405
WASHINGTON, D.C. 20006

Verso of Cover of 2nd Issue

Title Page of 1st Issue

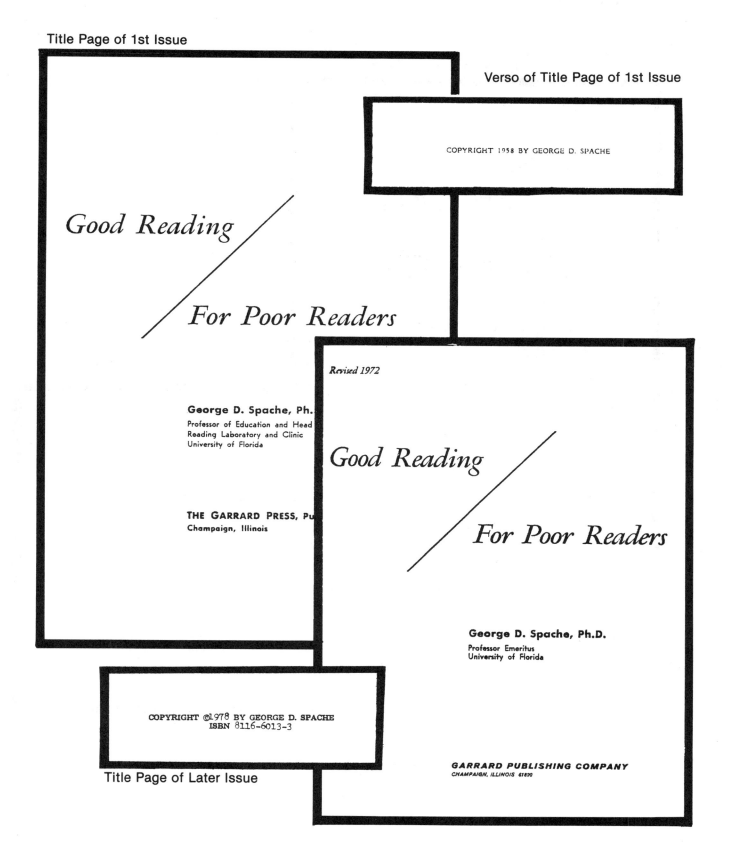

Verso of Title Page of 1st Issue

COPYRIGHT 1958 BY GEORGE D. SPACHE

Good Reading

For Poor Readers

Revised 1972

George D. Spache, Ph.
Professor of Education and Head
Reading Laboratory and Clinic
University of Florida

THE GARRARD PRESS, Pu
Champaign, Illinois

Good Reading

For Poor Readers

George D. Spache, Ph.D.
Professor Emeritus
University of Florida

COPYRIGHT ©1978 BY GEORGE D. SPACHE
ISBN 8116-6013-3

GARRARD PUBLISHING COMPANY
CHAMPAIGN, ILLINOIS 61820

Title Page of Later Issue

EXAMPLE S10

Title Page (Monographic Series)

STABILITY, SECURITY, AND CONTINUITY

Mr. Justice Burton and Decision-Making in the Supreme Court 1945-1958

MARY FRANCES BERRY

Contributions in Legal Studies, Number 1

GREENWOOD PRESS
WESTPORT, CONNECTICUT • LONDON, ENGLAND

Library of Congress Cataloging in Publication Data

Berry, Mary Frances.
    Stability, security, and continuity.

    (Contributions in legal studies; no. 1 ISSN 0147-1074)
    Bibliography: p.
    Includes index.
    1. United States. Supreme Court—History—20th century. 2. Burton, Harold Hitz, 1888-1964. 3. Judicial process—United States. I. Title. II. Series: Contributions in legal studies; no. 1.
KF8742.B47   347'.73'2634 [B]   77-84772
ISBN 0-8371-9798-8

Library of Congress Catalog Card Number: 77-84772
ISBN: 0-8371-9798-8
ISSN: 0147-1074

First published in 1978

Greenwood Press, Inc.
51 Riverside Avenue, Westport, Connecticut 06880

Printed in the United States of America

10 9 8 7 6 5 4 3 2 1

Verso of Title Page
(note ISBN & ISSN)

Example S1 (Serial): Changed Serial Title and Initialism as Title

> PJE : Peabody journal of education [text]. --
>   Vol. 48, No. 1 (Oct. 1970)-
>   Nashville, Tenn. : George Peabody College for
>   Teachers, c1970-
>   v. : ill. ; 24 cm.
>
>   Four times a year.
>   Running title: Peabody journal of education.
>   Continues: Peabody journal of education.
>   Also available in 35 mm., 16 mm., and microfiche formats,
> Ann Arbor, Mich. : University Microfilms.
>   ISSN 0167-956X = PJE. Peabody journal of education :
> $8.00 per year (libraries and organizations).
>
>   I. George Peabody College for Teachers.
>   II. Title: Peabody journal of education.

Pre-AACR 2

> PJE. Peabody journal of education.
>   v. 48-   Oct. 1970-
>   Nashville, Tenn., George Peabody College of Teachers.
>   v. ill. 24 cm. Quarterly.
>
>   Continues: Peabody journal of education.
>   Available on microfilm from University Microfilms.
>   Key title: PJE. Peabody journal of education, ISSN
> 0161-956X.
>
>   I. George Peabody College for Teachers, Nashville.
>   II. Title: Peabody journal of education.

(LC copy)

Discussion

Description:

Chief sources of information. The chief source of information is the title page. It displays the acronym and the title as well as other publication information.

Title and statement of responsibility area. AACR 2 does not address the issue of initials or acronyms standing for a journal title, either prominently displayed or preceding the expanded title. The title is transcribed according to Rule 1.1B1 with the expanded title treated as other title information. (Final interpretation of this area will be made when AACR 2 is being implemented and the library community begins to resolve questions not fully addressed or purposely left open.)

There is no statement of responsibility. Rule 12.1F3 clearly states that personal editors of a serial are given in a note but only if the cataloging agency considers a statement necessary.

Numeric and/or alphabetic . . . designation area. Volume 48, No. 1 begins a title change. The addition of "PJE" is considered a title change by the ISDS Center, and the journal was given a new ISSN and key title. The numbering of the journal continued, and this fact is reflected in the area.

Note area. The frequency note begins with a numeral. Numerals must be spelled out when they begin a note (see Appendix C.3). The expanded title is treated as a running title; it appears at the head of each page. The note is a formal note beginning with "Running title:." A formal note for a superseded title, in this case a title change, is always given when the earlier title is known (Rule 12.7B7 b).

Standard number and terms of availability. The new ISSN and the key title, which reflect the change of PJE, are given here. The terms of availability follow and the option to qualify these is taken. However, only the first subscription price was transcribed to illustrate the optional addition. Each library will have to decide whether it has the staff to transcribe this type of information, which is not only quickly outdated but also available from more current and reliable sources.

Access points:

Main entry. The application of Rules 21.1C and 21.7 make the journal also a title main entry.

Added entries. The teachers college as a corporate body appears to have a broader function exceeding publicational title. Since Rule 21.30E states that if in doubt provide an added entry for the body, added access was given. Rule 21.30J requires an added entry for a running title; other types of titles are also affected by this rule.

Example S2 (Serial): Cataloged from Later Available Issue / Record Contains Numeric/ Chronological Data

With Numeric and/or alphabetic, chronological or other designation area.

Family health [text]. -- Vol. 1, no. 1 (Oct. 1969)-
-- New York : Family Media, 1969-
v. : ill. (some col.), ports. ; 28 cm.

Monthly (Oct. 1969-June 1979), 10 issues yearly
(July/Aug. 1979-   )
Absorbed: Today's health, Apr. 1976.
Imprint varies.
Also available on microfilm: Ann Arbor, Mich. :
University Microfilms International, 1978-
ISSN 0014-7249 = Family health : U.S. $12.00 per year.
(Canada $13.00 per year; Foreign $14.00 per year)

Without Numeric and/or alphabetic, chronological or other designation area.

Family health [text]. -- New York: Family Media,
1969-
v. : ill. (some col.), ports. ; 28 cm.

Monthly (Oct. 1969-June 1979), 10 issues yearly
(July/Aug. 1979-   )
Absorbed: Today's health, Apr. 1976.
Imprint varies.
Also available on microfilm: Ann Arbor, Mich. : University
Microfilms International, 1978-
Description based on Vol. 8, no. 9 (Sept. 1976)
Began publication Oct. 1969. Cf. New serial titles.
ISSN 0014-7249 = Family health : U.S. $12.00 per year
(Canada $13.00 per yr.; Foreign $14.00 per yr.)

Pre-AACR 2

Family health. v. 1-   Oct. 1969-
[New York, Family Media, etc.]
v. illus. (part col.), ports. 28 cm. monthly.
Absorbed: Today's health, Apr. 1976.
Key title: Family health, ISSN 0014-7249.

(LC copy)

Discussion

Description:

Chief sources of information. The cover of the first available issue was used for the
bibliographic data. Some data will differ from the Pre-AACR 2 record since the publisher's
name has changed and other information on the serial title has become available, e.g., ISSN,
key title and microform publication data.

Title and statement of responsibility area. The title proper is transcribed as it appears on
the cover. The other title information, "incorporating Today's Health," is not given in this
area; it is transcribed in a note (see Rule 12.1E1).

Numeric and/or alphabetic . . . designation area. The first record does contain
numerical/chronological data but they are not taken from the first issue. AACR 2 instructions for this area are based on the availability of the first issue or volume of a serial; there
are provisions for the case of a library beginning its holdings with an issue other than the
first. (Although, as a rule, we are trying to adhere closely to the provisions of AACR 2 in
developing these samples and explanations, we feel that this problem required an exception
until such time as the lacuna is filled. LC has provided two answers (*RTSD Newsletter,* vol.
5, no. 2, 1980, p. 20), which are paraphrased below. We have provided a third.

1. Even though you are cataloging with a later issue in hand, give the enumeration of the first issue if that information is found in a reliable source (such as

NST, ULS, BUCOP, CONSER record in the OCLC data base or another reliable data base, etc.) and if you can assume that the first issue was used to supply the data. Use square brackets *only* if they are given in the source; otherwise *do not* use square brackets. (LC)

2. If you don't have a reliable source, *do not* give any enumeration; add a "Description based on" note and a "Began with" note. (LC)

3. Give the enumeration of the issue with which your subscription begins and add the "Description based on" note. (our suggestion)

The first record exemplifies the application of the first solution, and the next record the second solution. Note the "Description based on . . ." and "Began publication" note in the record.

Publication, distribution, etc. area. Even though the publisher is not a major one, the address has been omitted since it has changed and is mentioned in the note area as "imprint varies."

Note area. The notes display the change in frequency and also the fact that "Today's health" was absorbed. Changes in imprint are given in a generalized note. A "formats available" note is also given. The record without the numeric and/or alphabetic . . . designation area displays the "Description based on" and "Began publication" notes. Both records also have the ISSN, key title and terms of availability. (The option to provide the last item has been taken.) The subscription price varies depending on the location of the subscriber; three variant subscription prices from a later issue have been given. The rules are not specific on how to treat multiple terms of availability; thus the pattern established by AACR 2 and in the ISBDs has been followed.

Access points:

Main entry. Rule 21.1C requires entry under title when neither a personal nor corporate author can be determined.

Added entries. There are no added entries for this title.

Example S3 (Serial): Microfilm

> Family health [microform]. -- Vol. 7, no. 1 (Jan. 1975)-
> -- Ann Arbor, Mich. : University Microfilms International,
> 1978-
> microfilm reels : negative, ill. ; 35 mm. -- (Current
> periodicals series : publication ; no. 10,761)
>
> Also available in 16 mm. microfilm and microfiche formats: Ann
> Arbor, Mich. : University Microfilms International.
> Originally published: New York : Family Media, 1969-

Pre-AACR 2

> Family health, v. 1-   Oct. 1969-
> [New York, Family Media, etc.]
>   v. ill. (part col.) ports. 28 cm.
>
> Absorbed: Today's health, Apr. 1976.
> Microfilm. Ann Arbor, Mich., University
> Microfilms International. 1978-   reels,
> 35 mm. (Current periodical series, publication no.
> 10,761).

(not LC copy)

Discussion

Description:

Chief sources of information. The chief source is the title frame of the first microfilm available.

Title and statement of responsibility area. The title is that presented on the microfilm. There is no statement of responsibility and none should be constructed, according to Rule 1.1F2.

Numeric and/or alphabetic . . . designation area. The area gives the first volume and issue published in microfilm at the time of cataloging. Although vol. 1, no. 1 begins the title, regular publication of the microfilm serial starts with the later volume (see Rule 11.3B and 12.3B1). The data in the numeric and/or alphabetic . . . designation area is taken from the original. Rule 1.11A states: "Give data relating to the original in the note area (but give numeric and/or alphabetic, chronological, etc., designations of serials in the material [or type of publication] specific details area. . . .")

Publication, distribution, etc. area. AACR 2 catalogs the microform copy of an original as the microform (see 0.24). Therefore, the publication information reflects the microform publisher; the original publisher is given in a note (Rules 11.4B and 1.4B).

Physical description area. The extent of the item is given in terms of the microform; the rules governing this area are found in the microform chapter, Rule 11.5. The material designations are prescribed, and in this instance "microfilm" applies. The term may be shortened to "film" if the GMD is used. This option was not selected; the term is qualified by "reels."

Series area. The series of the microfilm publication is given in this area (see Rule 0.24, ". . . the starting point for description is the physical form of the item in hand . . ."). The form of the series is the same as given in the rules of 1.6, "Series area" (see Rule 11.6B1).

Note area. The other formats availability note is optional, as are most notes. The elements of the publisher's statement follow the format established for the area; the same prescribed punctuation is used (see Rule 12.7B16). The publication information about the original was given according to Rule 1.11A.

Access points:

Main entry. The main entry is under "title," according to Rule 21.1c 1.

Added entries. There are no added entries.

Example S4 (Serial): Superseded Serial (A)

Heat and fluid flow [text]. -- Vol. 1, No. 1 (Apr. 1971)-
v. 8, No. 2 (Oct. 1978). -- London ; Birmingham, Ala. :
Published by Mechanical Engineering Publications LTD,
for the Institution of Mechanical Engineers, 1971-1978.
8 v. : ill. ; 30 cm.

Two issues yearly.
Subtitle: The Journal of the Thermodynamics and Fluid
Mechanics Group of the Institution of Mechanical Engineers.
Continued by: The International journal of heat and fluid
flow. Mar. 1979.
ISSN 0046-7138 : £8.00 per year to members (£12.00 to non-
members in U.K. & Erie; £16.00 to non-members elsewhere).

I. Institution of Mechanical Engineers. Thermodynamics and
Fluid Mechanics Group.

Pre-AACR 2

Heat and fluid flow.
v. 1-8, No. 2; Apr. 1971-Oct. 1978.
[London, Birmingham, Ala., Mechanical
Engineering Publications LTD, for the Institution
of Mechanical Engineers]
8 v. ill. 30 cm. 2 no. a year.

"The Journal of the Thermodynamics and
Fluid Mechanics Group of the Institution
of Mechanical Engineers."
Superseded by: International journal of
heat and fluid flow, ISSN 0142-727X, Mar. 1979.
ISSN 0046-7138.

I. Institution of Mechanical Engineers, London.
Thermodynamics and Fluid Mechanics Group.

(LC copy—expanded record)

Discussion

Description:

Chief sources of information. The cover of the last issue of the superseded title and the cover of the first issue were used as the chief sources of information.

Title and statement of responsibility area. In such instances (cases) the second preferred source is the title page substitute—the cover (12.0B1). The other title information is not transcribed since it is lengthy and cannot easily be shortened; it is then supplied in a note (Rules 1.1E3 and 1.7B5/12.7B5). There is no statement of responsibility since the responsibility for the title is not readily apparent in the chief source of information (see Rule 1.1F2).

Numeric and/or alphabetic . . . designation area. The format of the data differs greatly from that utilized by previous rules, as the example of pre-AACR 2 cataloging illustrates. All data about the first issue are given together, with the chronological data in parentheses after the numeric information; the same applies to the closing data of this enumeration. The area is completed according to Rule 12.3F.
The abbreviation "Vol." is required at the beginning of any statement and before a roman numeral (see Appendix B9, footnote 14). However, when a volume designation must be given for the last volume of a serial, only the simple "v." is used.

Publication, distribution, etc. area. The place of publication and the publisher are taken from the contents page, one of the prescribed sources of information, and as such need not be placed in square brackets, as was the case in former rules. Both places of publication are transcribed since the first named is not located in the country of the cataloging agency (Rule 1.4C5 governs this case). The publication dates give the beginning date of publication and the closing date. Rules 12.4F3 and 1.4F8 treat the date element. The first named rule is precise in its requirement for giving the date of the last issue of the title; the latter makes this optional.

Physical description area. The record of a ceased serial gives the number of volumes which constitute the title. The specific material designation "v." is used for printed serials (12.5B1); serials in other physical formats have different specific material designations. The specific material designations should not be confused with the "numeric and/or alphabetic, chronological, or other designation area."

Note area. The notes contain the frequency of the serial (12.7B1) which was given, under earlier rules, with the extent of item. In the note area of this record the lengthy subtitle or other title information is given. Since an editorial page gives the title which supersedes the one we are working with, this information is given in a "Continued by:" note. Thus the user can be made aware that other issues are published under a different title. AACR 2 no longer uses the "Superseded by:" formal note when a changed title also begins a new numbering sequence.

Standard number and terms of availability. ISSN and key title do not appear in the item; they can be taken from any other source, however. Terms of availability are optional but have been transcribed as they appear on the contents page.

Access points:

Main entry. Without an attributable author or statement of responsibility the serial is entered under the title according to Rule 21.1C.

Added entries. The Thermodynamics and Fluid Mechanics Group is mentioned prominently in the subtitle, which is transcribed in the note area, so an added entry is provided for it according to Rule 21.30E.

Example S5 (Serial): Superseded Serial (B)

> The International journal of heat and fluid flow [text]. --
> Vol. 1, No. 1 (Mar. 1979)-   . -- London ; Birmingham,
> Ala. : Mechanical Engineering Publications, 1979-
> v. : ill. ; 30 cm.
>
> Quarterly.
> Published in consultation with the Thermodynamics and Fluid
> Mechanics Group of the Institution of Mechanical Engineers,
> Mar. 1979-
> Continues: Heat and fluid flow.
> ISSN 0142-727X = The International journal of heat and fluid
> flow : £8.00 per year to members (£18.00 to non-members)
>
> I. Institution of Mechanical Engineers. Thermodynamics and
> Fluid Mechanics Group.

Pre-AACR 2

> The International journal of heat and fluid flow.
> v. 1-   Mar. 1979-
> [London, Birmingham, Ala., Mechanical Engineering
> Publications]
> v. illus. 30 cm. quarterly.
>
> Vols. for 1979-   published in consultation with
> the Thermodynamics and Fluid Mechanics Group of the
> Institution of Mechanical Engineers.
> Supersedes: Heat and fluid flow.
> Key title: The International journal of heat and
> fluid flow, ISSN 0142-727X.
>
> I. Institution of Mechanical Engineers, London.
> Thermodynamics and Fluid Mechanics Group.

(LC copy)

Discussion

Description:

Chief sources of information. The first issue's cover under the new title was the chief source of information.

Title and statement of responsibility area. A separate record is made whenever the title proper has changed and the provisions of Rule 21.2C apply. In this instance "International journal of" was added the the title "Heat and Fluid Flow." The rule requires a new record when important words are added; these affect the retrieval of the title in either a manual or an online file. The title proper was taken from the cover, which is the chief source of information for the publication (Rule 12.0B1). A statement of responsibility is not part of the first area since it does not appear in the chief source of information nor is it otherwise easily discernible (1.1F2).

Numeric and/or alphabetic . . . designation area. The format of recording the numeric and chronological designation varies from the previous rules. "Vol. 1, No. 1" is recorded and followed by the date in parentheses; the hyphen follows the closing parentheses (Rule 12.3A1). The numeric and chronological designations are recorded as they appear on the item but standard abbreviations are employed (12.3C1). When a serial is actively published, the hyphen after the numerical and/or chronological designation is followed by four spaces before the next area is given (12.3B1); e.g., Vol. 1 (Mar. 1979)-

Publication, distribution, etc. area. Four spaces are left open following the publication date's hyphen (compare 12.4F1). For other information on this area see Example S4.

Note area. As in monographs, if the name of a group or person seems important enough to warrant an added entry, its relationship to the title must be given in a note. Here relationship of the Thermodynamics and Fluid Mechanics Group to the parent body and to the publication itself is given in the note, and an added entry is provided. The "Continues:" note relates this journal title to the previous one, even though its numbering is not continued.

Standard number and terms of availability area. The ISSN and the key title are taken from two different sources; the latter is taken from the CONSER (Conversion of Serials project) data base and the former from the title page. The key title is valid only when it has been assigned by the ISDS Center NSDP (National Serial Data Program). The terms of availability are taken from the item itself. Punctuation is prescribed by Rule 12.8.

Access points:

Main entry. Rule 21.1C providing for the title main entry was applied.

Added entries. Rule 21.30E provides for the added entry under the institution; this added entry has been justified by the second note.

Example S6 (Serial): Parallel Title

> Canadian journal of behavioural science [text] = Revue
>   canadienne des sciences du comportement. -- Vol. 1,
>   no. 1 (Jan 1969)-   . -- [Toronto] : Published for
>   the Canadian Psychological Association by University
>   of Toronto Press, 1969-
>   v. : ill. ; 23 cm.
>
> Quarterly.
> Text in English or French, English and French summaries.
> ISSN 0008-400X = Canadian journal of behavioural
> science : $7.50 per year ($2.00 single number).
>
> I. Canadian Psychological Association. II. Title:
> Revue Canadienne des sciences du comportement.

Pre-AACR 2

> Canadian journal of behavioural science. Revue
>   canadienne des sciences du comportement.
>   v. 1-   Jan. 1969-
> [Toronto] University of Toronto Press.
>   v. illus. 23 cm. quarterly.
>
> English or French; with summaries in English and French.
> Published for the Canadian Psychological Association.
> Key title : Canadian journal of behavioural science,
> ISSN 0008-400X.
>
> I. Canadian Psychological Association. II. Title:
> Revue canadienne des sciences du comportement.

(NLC [National Library of Canada] copy)

Discussion

Description:

Chief sources of information. If you were cataloging this title today, the title page of the first volume would serve as the chief source of information. The cover of the first issue is used as the chief source of information only when the title page is not available. Had this serial been cataloged at the time the first issue was published, the cover would be the chief source since the title page was published at a later date.

Title and statement of responsibility area. Cover and title page display both the English and French titles, and the text of the contributions to the journal is either in English or in

French; Rule 1.1D1, as referred to by Rule 12.1D1, was applied here since only one parallel title was involved.

Numeric and/or alphabetic . . . designation area. Numerical and chronological designations are printed on the cover and are transcribed as such, according to Rule 12.3C4; the prescribed punctuation for this rule must be determined by applying Rule 12.3A1.

Publication, distribution, etc. area. Detailed instructions for this area are found in the corresponding rules of Chapter 1 (Rule 1.4). The place of publication comes from outside the item and is placed in brackets. (Had any of the three sources which constitute the chief source of information for this area been used, brackets would not have been required.) The publisher's statement is also in two languages; in such cases the publisher's statement which matches the title proper should be transcribed as required by 1.4B5. The publisher's statement is transcribed as it appears on the cover; statements describing the publisher's function are included (Rule 1.4D3). Always refer to the general rules as instructed under the rules of an area for a specific format.

Note area. The fact that the title has text in two languages, English and French, is given in the note. The languages of the summaries are also given (see Rules 1.7B2 and 1.7B17, respectively).

Standard number and terms of availability area. ISSN and key title come from an outside source; the fact that these data did not appear in the item does not have to be indicated (Rule 12.0B1). The terms of availability is the subscription price at the time of cataloging rather than of the first issue. We decided that this information would be more useful and more accurate.

Access points:

Main entry. Although a corporate body is named on the cover and on the title page, the provisions under corporate body given in Rule 21.1B2 do not apply here. The main entry is under the title of the journal, according to 21.C2.

Added entries. Since the corporate body is named in the publication and appears to have a function beyond the publishing responsibility, an added access point is provided, applying Rule 21.30JE. Access is also provided to the parallel title since it differs significantly from the title proper. Rule 21.29B was applied; it permits an added entry under any title that may be used to approach a work.

Example S7 (Serial): Translated Serial

> Pharmaceutical chemistry journal [text]. --
> No. 1 (Jan. 1967)-No. 12 (Dec. 1970) ; Vol. 5,
> No. 1 (Jan. 1971)-   . -- New York : Consultants
> Bureau, 1967-
> v. : ill. ; 28 cm.

(cont'd.)

Monthly (Jan. 1967-   ), semimonthly (1976-   ).
Title also in Russian and its romanization.
Translation of: Khimiko-farmatsevticheskii zhurnal.
Numbering of issues for Jan. 1967-Dec. 1970 begins
each year with No. 1.
    Coden: PCJOAU.
    ISSN 0091-150X = Pharmaceutical chemistry
journal : $335.00 per year (1980-   ).

    I. Consultants Bureau.

Pre-AACR 2

Pharmaceutical chemistry journal.
    [v. 1]-   Jan. 1967-
    New York, Consultants Bureau.
        v. ill. 28 cm.

    A translation of Khimiko-
farmatsevticheskii zhurnal.
        Key title: Pharmaceutical chemistry
journal, ISSN 0091-150X.

    I. Consultants bureau.

(LC copy)

Discussion

Description:

Chief sources of information. Because of the absence of a title page the cover of the
first issue served as the chief source of information. The same source of information was
also utilized when the numbering designation changed.

Title and statement of responsibility area. The English translation of the title proper and
its original transliterated form appear on the cover of the first issue. Although these are
parallel titles, the original in transliterated form is recorded in a note, since the item does not
contain text in the original language, nor does the original title appear before the title proper
(1.1D3). A statement of responsibility is not required if 1.1F2 applies, as in this example
which does not display the statement of responsibility in the chief source of information.

Numeric and/or alphabetic . . . designation area. With volume 5, No. 1 the volume
designation changed from "no." to the volume and number designation and is identical with
the Russian original. According to Rule 12.3G, both designations should appear in the area;
the first one should give the beginning and closing date of the first enumeration. A space-
semicolon-space (;) separates the two elements.

Note area. The sequence of notes is fixed by Rule 12.7B, with frequency as the first
note. Changes in frequency are also recorded and the dates of the changes, when available,

are given (12.1B1). The parallel title is transcribed according to the provisions of Rules 1.1D3 and 12.7B5.

In the "Relationships with other serials" note, the original title is given in a formal note.

An explanatory note for irregular or complex numbering may be given (Rule 12.7B8). The note was added as an example on the assumption that the repetitive numbering may make retrieving a particular issue difficult.

Since there is no specific rule dealing with the transcription of the CODEN in a serial record, it was given as a formal note in the position of "Numbers" (12.7B19); it can be used for identification and retrieval.

Standard number and terms of availability. ISSN and the subscription price (i.e., terms of availability) are taken from two different sources; their prescribed sources are "any source."

Added access points:

Main entry. As with so many periodicals the entry is under title (Rules 21.1C 2, 21.7 and, for translations, 21.14B).

Added entries. An added entry is made for the publisher according to 21.30E, since he is responsible for the translation.

Example S8 (Serial): Corporate Main Entry

> National Advisory Council on Economic Opportunity.
>   Report [text] / National Advisory Council on
> Economic Opportunity. -- 9th (1977)-   . -- [Washington,
> D.C.] : The Council : [For sale by the Supt. of Docs.,
> G.P.O.], 1977-
>   v. ; 28 cm.
>
>   Annual.
>   Continues: National Advisory Council on Economic
> Opportunity. Annual report. 1967/68-1974/75.
>   Report year ends Mar. 31.
>   Supt. of Docs. no.: Y 3.Ec7/2: 1/
>
>   I. Title

Pre-AACR 2

> United States. National Advisory Council on Economic
>   Opportunity.
>   Report - National Advisory Council on Economic
> Opportunity. 9th-   1977-
> [Washington] National Advisory Council on Economic
> Opportunity.
>   v. 28 cm.

(cont'd.)

Continues: United States. National Advisory Council
on Economic Opportunity. Annual report - National Advisory
Council on Economic Opportunity.
Report year ends Mar. 31.
Supt. of Docs. no.: Y 3.Ec7/2: 1/

(not LC copy)

Discussion

Description:

Chief sources of information. The chief source of information is the cover of the first issue published under the new title.

Title and statement of responsibility area. The title "Report" is transcribed as it appears; however, the number preceding the title proper is dropped since it will vary from issue to issue (Rule 12.1B6). The statement of responsibility is transposed to its proper position as required by Rule 1.1F3.

Numeric and/or alphabetic . . . designation area. The area contains the numeric designation for the report and its date of coverage. Since the "9th" report is the first issue under the new title, the area begins with that number.

Publication, distribution, etc. area. The first issue does not contain any publication data; it is a copy of a typescript. Publication data are supplied from the "10th" report, its title page and verso, as the example indicates. The whole field is placed in square brackets. The corporate body is given in brief form since its full name appears in the statement of responsibility (see Rule 1.4D4). Note the change in the abbreviation of Govt. Print. Off.

Note area. After giving the frequency in the first note, the note explaining the relationship of the current serial title follows. The note is formal, and the data presented follow the pattern and the prescribed punctuation of the corresponding area's element of description (Rule 1.7A3, "Form of notes. Order of information"). A brief contents note gives the period covered by the report since it is different from the calendar year.

AACR 2 has a specific provision for numbers other than the ISSN or ISBN (Rules 1.7B19 and 12.7B19). This permits the transcription of the Supt. of Docs. number. The stock number was not given since it will change with each issue.

Access points:

Main entry. Rule 21.1B2 c justifies the corporate main entry. This rule addresses entry under corporate body for reports—the collective thought of the body.

Added entries. A title main entry was made, since the exceptions under 21.30J do not apply.

Example S9 (Serial): Personal Name Main Entry

> Spache, George D. (George Daniel), 1909-
>   Good reading for poor readers [text] / George D. Spache. --
> [1959]-   . -- Champaign, Ill. ; Garrard Press, c1958-
>   v. ; 26 cm.
>
>   Biennial.
>   ISSN 0162-7066 = Good reading for poor readers.
>
> I. Title.

Pre-AACR 2

> Spache, George Daniel, 1909-
>   Good reading for poor readers. [1st]-   ed. ; 1958-
> Champaign, Ill., Garrard Pub. Co.
>   v. ; 26 cm.
>   Key title: Good reading for poor readers, ISSN
> 0162-7066.
>
> I. Title.

(not LC copy)

Discussion

Description:

Chief sources of information. The title page of the first issue is the chief source of information for this serial.

Title and statement of responsibility area. Title and authorship are clearly defined and are recorded as such (see 12.1A1 and 12.1F1).

Numeric and/or alphabetic . . . designation area. Since there is no volume or part designation on the first issue, the date was given in square brackets. Later issues give the date on the title page. Only a chronological designation is given here (Rule 12.3D).

Publication, distribution, etc. area. The copyright date, preceded by "c" is recorded as the date element when the publication or distribution date is unknown (Rule 1.4F6).

Standard number and terms of availability. The issue does not contain an ISSN or key title. The ISBN is not transcribed.

Access points:

Main entry. The author, carrying the responsibility for the publication of the title, is treated as the main entry according to Rule 21.1A.

Added entries. According to Rule 21.30J, an added title entry is nearly always provided when the main entry is a personal or corporate name (for exceptions consult the rule).

Choice of treatment:

This example requires a brief explanation. The definition of a serial in AACR 2 has been liberally interpreted here. However, since AACR 2 permits entry of a serial under a personal name, the decision to treat the revisions of the title, which appear at regular biennial intervals serially, seemed economical and justified. We thought the title would also present an interesting example of a personal name entry serial.

Example S10 (Serial): Monographic Series
(Compare with Example M18)

> Contributions in legal studies. -- No. 1-
> -- Westport, Conn. : Greenwood Press, 1978-
> v. : ill. ; 22 cm.
>
> ISSN 0147-1074 = Contributions in legal studies.

Pre-AACR 2

> Contributions in legal studies.
> No. 1-   Westport, Conn., Greenwood Press
> 1978-
> v. : illus. 22 cm.
>
> Key title: Contributions in legal studies, ISSN
> 0147-1074.

(not LC copy)

Discussion

Description:

Chief sources of information. The title page is the chief source of information.

Title and statement of responsibility area. The title of this monographic publisher's series was used as the basis for the serial record. There is no statement of responsibility since, according to Rule 1.1F2, one should neither be constructed "nor extracted from the content of the item."

Publication, distribution, etc. area. Rule 12.4C, which covers the place of publication, refers to Rule 1.4C, which is also applied to serials. In this instance only the North American place name needs to be transcribed since the cataloging agency is situated in the United States. (See Rule 1.4B8 for a title which contains a multiple place and/or publisher or distributor.) In this example the location in Great Britain is not transcribed. The publisher's address is not added since we are dealing with a major trade publisher (Rule 1.4C7).

The date of publication is the publishing date from the verso of the title page, i.e., preliminaries which, as a chief source of information for this area, do not require brackets, as they did in previous rules.

Physical description area. The specific material designation for the extent of item of a printed serial is "v." even though the numeric designation is "no." in the sample (Rule 12.5B1). When volume numbers cannot be supplied because the item is still being received, three leading spaces are added before the "v." (see also Rule 1.5B5).

Note area. Monographic series do not require a note indicating that each issue also has its own title (Rule 12.7B4, paragraph 2). The note, "Each issue has a distinctive title," is used only for serials and not for monographic series.

Standard numbers and terms of availability area. The order of the elements in this area has changed with AACR 2. The new sequence is: ISSN, key title, terms of availability (cost) and qualifications. An equal sign (=) separates the ISSN and the key title. The ISBN is not recorded in the Standard number . . . area. (See Rule 1.8B2, which states: "If an item bears two or more such numbers, record the one which applies to the whole item, or applies to the item being described.")

Access points:

Main entry. The title is a publisher's series and as such carries no statement of responsibility. Rule 21.1C 1 was applied since no authorship could be determined.

Added entries. The title page provides the publisher as another possible access point; however, Rule 21.30E, which could be applied, prohibits an added entry under "publisher" if his sole function was the publication of the title, which is clearly the case here.

VII

Choice of Main Entry

The previous chapter has demonstrated that rules of description have been changing since AACR 1 was first published in 1967. Some of the changes were issued as supplements to later printings of these rules and others were made public through the Library of Congress *Cataloging Service Bulletin*. In the same manner, the choice of main entry has not remained static; these transformations have been less publicized but they too were published in the *Bulletin*.

For those who have worked with the fabled *Red Book* (*ALA Cataloging Rules for Author and Title Entries*) and even for those nurtured only on AACR 1, a historical perspective to these changes may make them more palatable. The changes are neither arbitrary nor malicious decisions. The new rules reflect a spirit of international cooperation and are another move toward universal bibliographic control. The Paris Principles of 1961 provide the framework for changes in choice and form of main entry headings, just as the ISBD does for description.

In the Paris Principles, two concepts—entry under corporate body and expanded use of title main entry—formed a bridge between two opposing points of view. The Anglo-American concept of corporate authorship or responsibility was more tightly defined and was accepted by a number of countries which had previously rejected it and by others which had applied it in a very limited manner. The principle of the title as the main entry when either a compiler or an editor had the responsibility for the work also was officially accepted at the conference as was the provision of successive entry for serial title.[1] It may be a consolation that after 20 years these principles are coming to fruition in the *Anglo-American Cataloging Rules,* 2nd edition.

ARRANGEMENT OF RULES

One very important change in AACR 2, more of format than content, is that all rules dealing with bibliographic access to a record have been consolidated under Chapter 21,

Choice of Access Points, which includes main and added entries. Although the main entry concept continues in the code, it no longer has the importance attributed to it in the past. Its correct choice is of importance in personal names, to collocate under the same name works published by one individual, and in single-entry bibliographies (bibliographies which provide only one access point to an item). If there is doubt as to what, or who, specifically constitutes the main entry, an access point (i.e., added entry) for the name or group will serve the patron just as well as a main entry would. The importance of cataloging is to provide access to an item owned by a library; our aim should be to afford staff and patrons a quick response to a catalog query. Predictability and understanding bibliographic conventions in various subject fields are important assets for librarians.

The rules for access to bibliographic records are presented in a similar manner to those for description. First is the "Basic Rule" (Rule 21.1), which presents the three types of access points: (1) Personal name, (2) Corporate body and (3) Title. The provisions for changes in title and changes in responsibility, including the form of the name, follow in Rules 21.2 and 21.3. Rule 21.2C covers change in a serial title. These three broad guidelines are the underpinnings of the rules for main entry; they are followed by the rules dealing with specific problems of entry. Some of the problems are illustrated by the examples in Chapter VI of this guide. Several of these examples are referred to below.

ENTRY UNDER TITLE

As implied above, more items are entered under title than occurred under AACR 1 and older rules. The affected AACR 1 rules are 3 and 4, "Works produced under editorial direction" and "Collections," respectively. The changes in these two chapters were published in 1975 in *Cataloging Service Bulletin,* no. 112. In AACR 2 a more precisely defined personal authorship, or responsibility for the intellectual or artistic content of an item, justifies the elimination of editors from consideration as main entry (see Rules 21.7 and 21.1C and Example M6). The only compiler considered responsible for the content of a work is the compiler of a bibliography (Rule 21.1A1). AACR 2 also expands authorship to include performers. (See Rules 21.1A1 and 21.23C and compare the AACR 2 and pre-AACR 2 records in Example SR1.) The specifications for transcriptions of performers in the statement of responsibility for sound recordings (Rule 6.1F1) aid in understanding when the performer is the main entry.

AACR 2 specifies requirements for entry under title in Rule 21.1C. Under 21.1C3, those materials formerly entered under the corporate body are treated as title main entries. (Compare the two sample records in Example M20.) A complementary rule is 21.30C, "Corporate bodies," which requires an added access point under the body's name if its responsibility goes beyond that of publisher. Thus we have not lost retrievability of the item, only shifted its main access point to the title.

ENTRY UNDER CORPORATE BODY

As illustrated in Example M20, the main entry under corporate body has been restricted to five categories: (1) materials of an administrative nature recording the activities of the corporate body and its staff; (2) laws, governmental regulations, court, decisions, treaties, etc., of governments or courts; (3) reports of commissions, etc., which record the collective thought of the body; (4) proceedings, minutes of conferences or other meetings, or the collective activities of a group, such as an expedition, when it is prominently named in the chief source of information; and (5) the collective activity of a performing group in sound recordings, films, video recordings (see Rule 21.1B2). Entry under a subordinate or related body is not treated in Chapter 21, although AACR 1, Rule 18, provides for this condition. The choice of name, subordinate or related, is addressed in Chapter 24 (Headings for Corporate Bodies).

Entry under subordinate or related body is specified in Rule 21.1B4, but it is tied directly to Rule 21.1B2, which determines when a work should be entered under a corporate body. To apply the rules correctly, it is essential to also consider the form of the corporate name (Rules 24.12-24.15) and the rules for government bodies and officials (Rules 24.17-24.26). Similar rules for religious bodies and officials exist also and must be followed when applicable.

An item entered under a corporate body applying AACR 2's rules would always have had a corporate main entry under AACR 1. Example S6 (serial) is an annual report to which Rule 21.1B2c applies. Another report example is M10, which is also entered under a corporate body, a commission, by applying the same AACR 2 rule. However, Example M11, also a report, is entered under the first personal name on the title page, according to Rule 21.6B, "Principal responsibility not indicated," since none of the provisions under 21.1B were appropriate. The example indicates no change here either; AACR 1, Rule 17A1, "Works of Corporate Authorship," also requires entry under the personal name for this title.

A large variety of materials continues to be entered under the corporate body. Rule 21.4B, "Works emanating from a single corporate body," clarifies Rule 21.1B2 for entry under corporate body; 21.1B2 must apply before 21.4B takes effect. Under this latter rule, such familiar problems as museum or gallery catalogs continue to be entered under the name of the organization responsible for the exhibit.

Meetings and conferences are other types of publications which are entered under the corporate name (i.e., conference name) under Rule 21.1B2d. However, the clause "provided that the conference, expedition or event is prominently named in the item being cataloged" must be observed. The definition of "prominently named" (see Rule 0.8) determines whether or not the entry is under the conference name. The definition requires a formal statement in the primary source of information for the title and statement of responsibility area or for the edition area. In Example M6, the conference is entered under the title because the primary source of information does not contain a formal statement naming the conference. Example M7, in comparison, has its main access point under the conference name, which appears as a formal statement on the title page (a monograph's primary source of information for the title and statement of responsibility area).

UNIFORM TITLES

Headings formalized by librarians have been eliminated to a large extent; those remaining are uniform titles. Therefore, we find that the entry "Jews. Liturgy and ritual." has been dropped in AACR 2 along with the form subheading "Liturgy and ritual." The word "Jews" in the first part of the heading could never be justified since it defines individuals whose faith is Judaism, not a church or denominational body. The entry therefore yields to the uniform title for the liturgical work. The form subheading was also added to the heading for a church or denominational body (AACR 1, Rule 29), e.g., "Catholic Church. Liturgy and ritual." AACR 1 gives as the primary rationale for the continued use of the form subheading "the long-established usage of this form."[2]

The examples below illustrate the change in access to these materials; the new heading and its uniform title will interfile with all other works entered under the name of the religious body.

    AACR 1:   Catholic Church. Liturgy and ritual
                      [Caeremoniale Romanum]

    AACR 2:   Catholic Church.
                      [Caeremoniale Romanum]

    AACR 1:   Jews. Liturgy and ritual.
                      Haggadah of Passover . . .

    AACR 2:   Haggadah.
                      Haggadah of Passover . . .

In these examples the uniform title acts as the device to bring works of a specific group together. The form subheading "Liturgy and ritual" is not applied in AACR 2, but the uniform title, which was added as well under AACR 1, continues to form part of the entry (Rule 21.39).

Laws and Government Publications

The entry for laws and certain government publications, as mentioned under AACR 2, Rule 21.1B2b (e.g., decrees, administrative regulations, treaties, court decisions, hearings, etc.), mixes the rules for access points and their form since for this type of material a librarian is often forced to create a heading and devise a uniform title. We will attempt to keep these separate. AACR 2 has dropped all form subheadings for these materials, and the entry is the jurisdiction or the country to which these rules and regulations apply. The uniform title is used to bring the laws or codes of a jurisdiction or governmental body together in a file, as shown by the following:

    AACR 1:   Boston. Ordinances, local laws, etc.

    AACR 2:   Boston.
                      [Laws etc.]

    AACR 1:   Richmond, Va. Ordinances, local laws, etc.
                      Building code of the city of Richmond, Vir-.
                      ginia . . .

AACR 2:   Richmond, (Va.)
           [Building code]
           Building code of the city of Richmond,
           Virginia . . .

AACR 1:   United States. Constitution.
           The Constitution of the United States . . .

AACR 2:   United States.
           The Constitution of the United States . . .

There is neither a form division nor a uniform title for such documents as constitutions or charters.

These are just a few of the changes relating to the main entry for laws and related official publications. We will consider the problem of the form for these headings further in Chapter VIII.

SUPPLEMENTARY WORKS

The AACR 1 provision which permitted the recording of a supplementary work on the same bibliographic record (Rule 19A, second sentence, and Rule 155) has been abandoned. LC implemented this change as early as 1975 and published the details in *Cataloging Service Bulletin,* no. 119, 1976. Dependent or related works are entered under their appropriate heading with a "name-title added entry or other added entry," relating the work to the parent work. Thus, these works will be linked in a file, such as a card catalog. The description of these titles is treated under Rule 1.1B9, or as specified under a particular format. For serials the rules are 12.1B3-5.

NAME-TITLE REFERENCES

Initialisms or abbreviated names are not treated as added entries in AACR 2 but become name-title references (Rule 26.2B2). AACR 2 avoids the term "author" so studiously that we no longer have a corporate author but deal in corporate bodies. The all-inclusiveness and the general application of Chapter 21 seem to necessitate this change. The formats are not limited to written material, to which we commonly apply the term "author." Its original Latin meaning, "originator or producer," would serve nicely in the context of the rules; but this meaning is lost and we must deal with the cumbersome "statement of responsibility."

* * * *

These are the highlights of the changes for main entry. There are numerous smaller changes, which can be identified with Hagler's *Where's That Rule?* (see Chapter IX). As emphasized previously, once the basic concepts are understood the specific rules will be easier to learn and apply; it is more important to know there are special provisions and to seek these out whenever we need them. Usage will better acquaint us with the new code, and applying it daily will be the best teacher.

VIII

Major Changes in Forms of Names

The changes discussed in the previous chapters can all easily be absorbed in the daily work flow and the catalogs. However, on the ominous Day One, January 2, 1981, we will not only adopt the changes in record format and AACR 2 choices of access points, but we must also adopt AACR 2 forms of names. We will have to make names already established in our catalogs compatible with these new forms. This is a twofold labor, since many libraries superimposed AACR 1 rules on their existing catalogs. The Library of Congress instituted the concept of superimposition to alleviate the impact of AACR 1 on catalogs and catalog departments.* The task before us is Herculean.

MAKING PLANS FOR CHANGE

As we must do in making decisions on levels of description, we must again analyze our individual situations; that is, each library must assess its priorities, the amount of staff time available and the day-to-day work which must be continued, and then relate these to the anticipated changes.

Estimating the Amount of Change

However, before we decide how to absorb AACR 2 changes in forms of names, we must try to quantify them. Two methods may be used to estimate the amount of change a catalog requires. One is to take a given period of catalog record production and to examine the name headings and uniform titles for their compliance with AACR 2. The sample should be large enough to be valid. Two weeks to one month of production would appear sufficient; the time span selected essentially depends on the volume of material processed. This

---

*Under superimposition only new names were formulated according to AACR 1; names established under previous rules continued in use, often resulting in split files for corporate name headings.

method can determine the number and types of headings requiring adjustment, as well as how the new forms will be merged in the present catalog. At the same time, as the names are being checked against the catalog, one can also determine the number of cards per heading which will need to be altered. From ongoing catalog maintenance activities we can easily determine the time required and the cost of making the changes. Thus we arrive at:

- The rate of change, particularly in the initial months (i.e., the number of names which result in conflict and change).

- The types of names affected.

- The average number of cards which must be changed per affected heading.

- The time required to make the change, as well as its cost.

This method appears to be most useful if systematic change is not planned, and if only those headings are changed which would create a conflict between the AACR 2 form of the name and the pre-AACR 2 one. However, it is essential to decide how to deal with headings for universities and other bodies with numerous subdivisions or with laws and other material which have form subdivisions no longer in use in AACR 2. There are several alternatives:

- Change only those headings with subordinate units for which new material is added.

- Change the complete file. Here two approaches are possible: (1) change at first only the affected headings and make a record for reworking the file later, or (2) change all headings when the first conflicting heading is discovered.

- Make references to and from the various forms for the same body or category of material.

Each solution has its merits, its positive and negative effects on service and usage of the catalogs.

The other method is a statistical sampling of names in the catalog, as was done by the Library of Congress and also by William Potter.[1] This will give an estimated total number and the kinds of headings that may require change. It is particularly useful if a systematic changeover to AACR 2 is desired and can estimate the number of cards that must be changed per heading. If a new AACR 2 catalog is planned, with links between the old and the new one, it can also provide the number of terms which will require linking references between these catalogs. We will also need to test the time required to make the links by working through a number of headings for which links are required. At the same time, we must determine the level of staff competency necessary to perform the work. We will thus also be able to estimate cost figures. By this method, we arrive at:

- The estimated number of headings in the catalog which will be different from the AACR 2 form.

- The types of headings requiring change.

- The average number of cards per heading which must be changed.

- The time and cost required to perform this task.

The two methods complement each other and both determine the impact of AACR 2 on the present catalog. Knowledge of the rate of change is necessary to plan for dealing with the initial impact of the new code on the catalog and how to prevent deterioration of service to staff and users. Knowing the number of changes required can aid in the initial decisions on which route to pursue—either to close the current catalog and begin a new one, or to change all headings to the AACR 2 form.

Short-term Solutions

It appears self-evident that the initial months will result in a larger number of changes. These will vary from one type of library to another, depending on the size of the collection and the acquisitions program.[2] As time passes most libraries will experience a drop in the quantity of changes required when new cards are filed and only those headings are changed which have created a conflict. With some planning, we can alleviate AACR 2's initial impact and provide some short-range solutions.

A library may choose to: (1) make a nicely retyped correction, at the expense of making other needed corrections or of getting records returned to the catalog; (2) cancel now superfluous data in headings, interfiling or using guidecards wherever feasible; (3) have temporary split files when numerous cards are filed under the same heading; or (4) for example, underline the first number of a conference date which under the new rules has become the second filing element after the conference title.

All of the above constitute a patchwork technique. (Some of these solutions were outlined by Hewitt and Gleim in early 1979.[3]) It may be desirable in many situations to keep records of some of the "patches" so as to make the complete change at a later date, particularly for those libraries which do not have an online or COM catalog in their foreseeable future. The split file technique should be used sparingly, since it can inhibit use of material and make the already complex access tool to collection even more difficult to manipulate. No matter which approach is chosen, planning is essential and larger libraries should have many of these plans already in progress.

Some of the following techniques may save planning time and make the transition go more smoothly during the first year. With the aid of literary dictionaries or handbooks, many of the better known authors writing under pseudonyms can be identified. We can then make references and decide if the name heading should be changed or if all cards should be filed behind a guidecard. The catalog should contain an explanatory note giving the rationale for filing entries displaying the original name behind a guidecard with the pseudonym heading. Of course, there must be a reference from the form of the name no longer used to the one now in use. At a later date, when the pressure has lessened, the original name can be changed to the new form or the pseudonym.

If there are only a limited number of cards for a heading the records could be changed prior to Day One, especially since the pseudonym is also the preferred form under AACR 1.

The preparatory work can be done and the change made on January 2, 1981, or soon thereafter. In instances where such a name also appears in the tracings (i.e., the name is an added entry), the old form may remain in the tracings since a "see" reference should refer a staff member working with the record to the new form of the heading. Some examples for which change can be anticipated and preparations made are given below.

Old Form	AACR 2 Form
Samuel Langhorne Clemens	Mark Twain
Marie Henri Beyle	Stendhal
Jean Paul Friedrich Richter	Jean Paul
Amandine-Lucile-Aurore Dupin, baronne Dudevant	George Sand
Mary Ann Evans	George Eliot
Françoise Quoirez	Françoise Sagan

Other headings may be linked by "see also" references, with an explanatory note describing the split file. This is a cumbersome solution for library users and reference staff, but it is an immediate means to bridge the gap between new and old forms of headings. Some sample headings are:[4]

Old Form	AACR 2 Form
Alabama. Geological Survey	Geological Survey of Alabama
Boston. Museum of Fine Arts	Museum of Fine Arts (Boston)
* Chicago. University	University of Chicago
* North Carolina. University	University of North Carolina (Chapel Hill Campus)
* United States. Laws, statutes, etc.	United States. [Laws, etc.]
* United States. Laws, statutes, etc.	United States. [Bankruptcy law, 1938]

The items marked by asterisks represent two types of problems. University headings, as well as other corporate bodies, often have numerous subheadings; some of these may now be entered independently, while others may remain dependent. When no new acquisition uses one of these newer name forms as an access point, that name will continue under the old form of the heading. A user of the catalog could conceivably overlook a reference, particularly a general one, and consequently not locate pertinent material entered under the earlier form of the name. The items with the form subheadings for United States illustrate a second problem area, for which linking references should be used as a temporary measure only. Form subheadings have been abandoned for uniform titles; these translate to specific laws, acts, treaties, liturgies. These materials must be dealt with individually.

Being aware of these issues is half the resolution of the problem; split files are only a temporary solution, useful until a catalog can be replaced by COM products or by an online version. When the card catalog must be maintained for an unspecified period, these files must be merged and each heading must be converted to its new form.

Another method of dealing with some headings is to interfile them. This can be done when punctuation is dropped, when acronyms change from upper and lower case letters to all upper case, when the place name is deleted, or when the name of a larger administrative unit is added to a place name. Some examples of old and new names are:[5]

Old Form	AACR 2 Form
Baltimore. Museum of Art	Baltimore Museum of Art
Ernst and Ernst	Ernst & Ernst
Havana	Havana (Cuba)
Hongkong	Hong Kong
Howard University, Washington, D.C.	Howard University
Idaho. Bureau of Mines and Geology	Idaho Bureau of Mines and Geology
* India (Republic). Parliament	India. Parliament
Nato Advanced Study Institute	NATO Advanced Study Institute
* Organization for Economic Co-operation and Development	Organisation for Economic Co-operation and Development
Salvador	El Salvador
* Santa Barbara, Calif. Museum of Art	Santa Barbara Museum of Art
*** United Nations. Children's Fund	UNICEF
** United States. Air Force. 8th Air Force	United States. Air Force. Air Force, 8th
** United States. Army. 2d. Ranger Infantry Battalion	United States. Army. Ranger Infantry Battalion, Second

Those items preceded by one asterisk(*) may have the additional place name canceled in ink before the old form and the new are interfiled; no other work needs to be done. The orthographic change in "organization" could also be accomplished with a pen; the "z" easily becomes an "s." Both forms could also be interfiled without a change, but they should be preceded by an explanatory guidecard.

When the numeric changes its position in a heading as with "United States. Air Force. 8th Air Force" or for a conference, the initial letter of each filing word could be underlined, skipping the numeric and then placing it at the end of the sequence. Other temporary or not so temporary solutions come to mind quickly; the question is only whether we are willing to live with them in our catalogs.

In the example preceded by three asterisks (***), interfiling may be the most economic measure. Such cases can also be made split file headings; they will look neater and may be more readily consulted. A general policy should be established, one which also meets with the approval of the public service staff, but a clear understanding of the problems in either method is essential.

As already indicated, a pen can work wonders when parts of names need deletion. The following headings are candidates for this type of alteration.

Old Form	AACR 2 Form
American Society of Mechanical Engineers. Fluids Engineering Division. Fluid Mechanics Committee	American Society of Mechanical Engineers. Fluid Mechanics Committee
Aristotles	Aristotle
Battelle Memorial Institute, Columbus, Ohio, Pacific Northwest Laboratory, Richland, Wash.	Pacific Northwest Laboratory
Brontë, Emily Jane, 1818-1848	Brontë, Emily, 1818-1848
Degas, Hilaire Germain Edgar, 1834-1917	Degas, Edgar, 1834-1917
Kansas. State University of Agriculture and Applied Science, Manhattan	Kansas State University

These are a small number of headings. A local decision must determine whether or not canceling parts of the name no longer used is an acceptable means to accommodate change, particularly to keep the number of split files at a minimum.

There are some names or headings that must have additions or complex changes, for which neither method is very satisfactory. Although guidecards and interfiling can be utilized in many situations, the danger of excess is great; files must be maintained and be usable. The situation can become chaotic if too many headings with variant forms of a name are interfiled. There are numerous solutions, but decisions must now be made. They must be made rapidly, with a long-range view, so that we can be ready on Day One, or shortly thereafter.

THE RULE CHANGES

Many of the foregoing examples will not be reflected in the following discussion of changes in the rules. The reason is quite simple; the examples indicate 13 years of superimposition: the maintaining of forms obsolete since the publication of AACR 1 in 1967.

Personal Names

A brief analysis of the structure for personal name headings in AACR 1 and AACR 2 will help us understand the use and application of these rules. When the two texts are juxtaposed we observe that a number of AACR 1 rules have been divided into smaller segments and are given as separate rules. For example, hyphens and diacritics are not treated as part of spelling; they have been separated from "Choice and Form of Names" (AACR 1) and are included in AACR 2 21.1, "General Rules." This has a positive and negative affect. On the positive side, the AACR 2 rules are more clearly defined and can be consulted with more facility; on the negative side, they require from the cataloging librarian a more detailed understanding of the elements of name headings and a greater awareness of their structure.

Initially the structure appears to be identical. The table of contents is very similar, with one minor exception, as follows:

AACR 1	**AACR 2**
1. Choice and Form of Name	1. Choice of Name
2. Entry of Name	2. Entry Element
3. General Additions to Names	3. Additions to Names
Special Rules for Names in	4. Special Rules for Names of
Certain Languages*	Certain Languages

A closer examination reveals that there are not only changes in the titles for each section; there are also changes in content. While the older rules frequently mix choice and form of names, AACR 2 attempts to be more consistent and reference is greatly facilitated. Most notable is the expansion of "Additions to Names," which now also include titles of nobility, honor, etc.; saints and spirits. In AACR 1 only "Date" and "Distinguishing terms" are included.

Form of name

Of greater interest are those changes that affect the form of a personal name. Two are presented in the general rules. Initials are the preferred choice if the person is "commonly known" by these.

    Example: H.D.
not   Hilda Doolittle

The hyphen (-) is retained when it appears in a person's given name.

    Example: Jean-Paul Sartre
not   Jean Paul Sartre

The general rules are then amplified by specific rules for the various choices of names.

The principle for choice is a person's most commonly known name or form of name. It is not different from that of AACR 1. However, the new code's guidelines for determining "most commonly known" have changed the order of preference, which is as follows:

1. The most frequently found form in a person's work, which is either
   a) taken from the chief source of information of the works published in his or her language,[6] or
   b) for persons responsible for nonverbal works (e.g., photographers, motion picture producers, sculptors) the name "commonly known from reference sources[†] issued in his or her language or country of residence or activity." (Rule 22.1B), or

2. The most frequently found form of the name in reference sources, or

3. The latest form.

---

*This subsection of 3. now has independent status in AACR 2.

[†]AACR 2 includes books and articles about a person as reference sources.

The order of preference has been reversed; reference sources had been the preferred choice for establishing a name under AACR 1.

The principle for choice of name also governs its fullness. The fullest form appearing in a prominent position is required by AACR 1; AACR 2 requires the "most commonly found" form of the name. If, however, the predominant form cannot be ascertained, the second choice is the latest form and the third choice is the fullest form.[7] The implications are that unused initials and given names are dropped.

Example: Wolfgang Amadeus Mozart
not   Johann Chrysostom Wolfgang Amadeus Mozart

Pseudonyms

The rule for pseudonym as choice for a name was established in the earlier code; AACR 2 adds changes. When a person uses more than one name for his or her work, the preferred choice is no longer the real name, but rather the form used in the latest editions of the person's work. When there is no predominant name, each item will be entered under the name appearing on it, the alternative rule in AACR 1.[8]

Selection of entry element

The rules for the selection of the entry element have minor changes only. The breakdown is more detailed and there are clarifications and requirements for references. Changes in the rules for entry under title of nobility affect the filing element only; surname and title are no longer placed at the end of the name. The title stands alone after the comma.

Example: Macaulay, Thomas Babington Macaulay, Baron
not   Macaulay, Thomas Babington, Baron Macaulay

A comma is inserted after a person's name consisting of a given name only and identified by "words or phrases denoting place of origin, domicile, occupation, or other characteristic that are commonly associated with the name" (Rules 22.8A and 22.15A).

Examples: John, the Baptist
not   John the Baptist

      Alexander, of Aphrodisias
not   Alexander of Aphrodisias

This form is analogous to that for entry under surname (Rule 22.15A); by increasing consistency in the treatment of names the catalogs may eventually be more user-oriented. As noted earlier, AACR 2 permits the use of initials as choice for names and the use of "a characterizing word or phrase, or a phrase naming another work by a person, in direct order" (Rule 22.11D).

Names in nonroman alphabet

Names in a nonroman script have also been changed again. The major change came with AACR 1 in 1967 when it became acceptable to enter such a name in the form as it appears in an author's work, except for names in the Cyrillic alphabet. Rule 22.3C makes no exception and greatly simplifies the rules. In cases of entry under given name the form established in English-language reference sources predominates, and the preference for names entered under surname is the "romanized form according to the table for the language adopted by the cataloguing agency." Additional provisions permit establishing the name as given in the work. LC has adopted the alternative Rule 22.3C2 for persons entered under surname and will establish the name as found in English-language reference sources.[9]

In the music and sound recording examples (see Chapter VI), both results are illustrated. Examples MU3 (Shostakovich, Dmitri) and SR4 (Tchaikovsky, Peter Ilich) give the form as established in English-language reference sources. However, in SR4 the added entry "II. Nesterenko, Evgenii" gives the romanized form according to the ALA/LC table. The name could not be verified in the available reference sources and was therefore given in a form different from that in the note area of the record.

Additions to names

The additions to names have been expanded, although in AACR 1 these often were considered parts of the names. Formerly abbreviated titles for "Bishop" and "Archbishop" are given in full form. The term "Spirit" has become an identifying element for names since AACR 2 also extends "intellectual and artistic responsibility" (i.e., authorship) to spirits (Rules 21.26 and 22.14). These are only minor changes in the transformation of this section. Now it includes titles of honor, nobility and address; saints; additions to names entered under surname or given name; and popes and other ecclesiastical officials. When initials form part of the name, the full name or names may be added in parentheses:

Example: Cummings, E.E. (Edward Estlin), 1894-1962.

Rule 22.16A requires this form only when one name must be distinguished from another; the same concept applies to the addition of dates.

The situations when a cataloging librarian may add distinguishing terms have been limited. Terms are added in parentheses when the name is a given name, but are preceded by a comma when the name is a surname. Identifying words or phrases are not added to surnames unless they are taken from the item or from a reference source. Works by different authors with identical names are interfiled "if neither dates nor distinguishing terms are available" (Rule 22.20). As stated above, LC will add the full name and the dates whenever that information is readily available.

These are the major changes which will affect the personal names in a catalog or other bibliographic file. They are not drastic and would be absorbed with facility had libraries opted to accept AACR 1 changes in 1967.

Corporate Bodies and Geographic Names

Although AACR 2 gives geographic names a separate chapter, they are also discussed in Chapter 24 with corporate names since they are used in conjunction with them.

Choice of geographic names

The choice for the form of geographic names is the English form when one is in general use; the vernacular form is used if an English form cannot be established. LC will also select the English form rather than follow the Board of Geographic Names (BGN) in those instances when the Board has established the vernacular one. LC has also reported that it will use "Soviet Union," *not* "Union of Soviet Socialist Republics" and will also continue with "Great Britain" for "United Kingdom," the preferred form in AACR 2.[10]

New to geographic names is Rule 23.3, which deals with changes of names. In essence, this is the concept of successive entry: use that name which is correct at the time of the original publication and distribution of the item as indicated in the source data.

Additions to place names

Additions or qualifiers to place names are always placed in parentheses; this application of parentheses is new. Generally the larger geographic entity is added to a place name in order to distinguish between identical names. AACR 2 Appendix B contains a list of sanctioned abbreviations. The rules require that the name of a state or country be added to all cities. The examples below illustrate the implications of this rule change.

Old Form	AACR 2 Form
Antwerp	Antwerp (Belgium)
Cairo	Cairo (Egypt)
Chicago	Chicago (Ill.)
Milan	Milan (Italy)
New York (City)	New York (N.Y.)

In addition, the order of the larger and smaller jurisdictions displayed together has changed. Under AACR 1 the smaller unit was added to differentiate between identical place names and countries; now the smaller precedes the larger.

Old Form	AACR 2 Form
Friedburg, Ger. (Bavaria)	Friedburg (Bavaria, Germany)
Friedburg, Ger. (Hesse)	Friedburg (Hesse, Germany)

The application of the rules is very consistent and logical and should be much easier to apply with consistency.

Choice of corporate body names

Chapter 24 (Headings for Corporate Bodies) experienced a transformation similar to that for the chapter on personal names. The table of contents, however, is radically different from that in AACR 1. Its construction reflects the AACR 2 conceptualization of rules structure, from general to specific, and should aid both the experienced and inexperienced librarian. Predominance of form on items issued by the organization links this chapter's choice for form of name to that for personal names. Additions to the rules have changed some of them drastically; in other cases deletions have had a similar effect; and other rules have been clarified to facilitate their consistent application.

The basic rules eliminate the restriction of entry under a body's initials when these are in all upper case letters and also eliminate the full stop (period) after each letter, unless they are used predominantly. However, spaces between letters are always removed (e.g., AFL-CIO, *not* A.F.L.-C.I.O. or A F L - C I O). When variant forms of name enter into the decision process and the chief sources of information contain more than one form of the name, two factors are to be considered. Select:

1. The form of name as it appears in the chief source of information, or

2. The briefest form when variant forms appear in the chief source of information.

The impact of these changes is illustrated by the following examples, including a few from LC's *Cataloging Service Bulletin,* nos. 6 & 8.

Old Form	AACR 2 Form
American Concrete Institute	ACI Committee 214
American Welding Society. Committee on Definitions and Symbols	AWS Committee on Definitions and Symbols
Institute of Electrical and Electronics Engineers. Power Group	IEEE Power Group
World Health Organization	WHO
North Atlantic Treaty Organization	NATO

Thus, predominant usage and the preference for using the brief form of a name under AACR 2 (Rules 24.1 and 24.2D) will replace many long names with their acronyms or abbreviations.

Additions to corporate body names

The rules for treatment of geographic or place names also affect additions to names of corporate bodies, but they do not follow the pattern absolutely:

1. The larger jurisdiction or geographic entity is not added to the more specific one when it is part of the name of the corporate body.

2. The name of the most specific local political jurisdiction in which the body is located is added.

These are the two major rules of the seven which deal with the addition of the place name for the identification of the body. When two governing jurisdictions have identical names, differentiating place names are also added (Rule 24.6). These additions include not only the name of the next larger jurisdiction but, when necessary, also the type of jurisdiction. There are, of course, the customary additions of dates, institutions and general designations in English. All these are placed in parentheses when added to a corporate name. The rules of omission have not changed.

The order and punctuation of the elements added to a conference name have been altered. The date precedes the place but follows the number.

Old Form	AACR 2 Form
Louisiana Cancer Conference, 2d, New Orleans, 1958	Louisiana Cancer Conference (2nd : 1958 : New Orleans)

All identifying elements are placed in parentheses and each element except the first is preceded by a space-colon-space (:).

Government Names

The selection of the name of a government is ruled by a conventional concept comparable to that of the predominant or established form of name used in so many other cases in AACR 2. This is not new to AACR 2, specifically; the first edition contained the same provisions. Only the above mentioned changes for additions to geographic names and those of Rule 24.6 will apply here. The following examples illustrate the changes:

Old Form	AACR 2 Form
Berlin (West)	Berlin (Germany : West)
Berlin (East)	Berlin (Germany : East)
Pisa	Pisa (Italy)
Pisa (Province)	Pisa (Italy : Province)
Quebec (City)	Quebec (Quebec)
Quebec (Province)	Quebec (Canada : Province)
Quebec (County)	Quebec (Canada : County)

The changes in punctuation illustrated above are also seen in the formulation of headings for government officials and heads of state. The personal name of the official and the dates of office are placed in parentheses, with the name preceded by a space-colon-space (:). For example:

Old Form	AACR 2 Form
U.S. President, 1961-1963 (J.F. Kennedy)	United States. President (1961-1963 : Kennedy)

The name is now given in a brief form only, i.e., the surname alone. The change facilitates machine filing. (In most manual filing, people are instructed to ignore initials preceding a surname. A machine is unintelligent and files character by character, unless it is programmed to do otherwise—which may be a costly and time-consuming process.)

Subordinate Bodies

The general rule for subordinate and related bodies (Rule 24.12) begins with a positive statement: Enter a subordinate body . . . or related body directly under its name . . . unless. . . This statement is lacking in AACR 1. The results are seen in the following name changes made by the Library of Congress and issued in its *Cataloging Service Bulletin,* nos. 6 & 8:

Old Form	**AACR 2 Form**
Gothenburg, Sweden. Universitetet. Historiska institutionen.	Historiska institutionen i Göteborg
Organization for European Cooperation. European Productivity Agency	European Productivity Agency

The specific rules which follow 24.12 tighten the liberal regulations. The rules for government bodies parallel those for corporate bodies. Both sets of rules refer to the basic rules which govern this chapter and in which "predominantly identified" and "predominant usage" are given as criteria for establishing a name. Restraints are added and, as always, the more specific rules assist in arriving at a name according to AACR 2.

UNIFORM TITLES

This chapter has brought together all rules governing uniform titles. The structure again follows that of the code, first giving the overall principles for the use of uniform titles and then presenting the specialized rules. Chapters VI and VII of this guide discussed the changes in these rules.

Uniform titles are, more than anything else, filing devices which permit a library to file together different editions of the same work issued under variant titles and thus make the library user aware of the variant issues in the collection. In the case of laws, a subject arrangement was created under the old rules in the author or title file. Even the new code does not fully do away with this phenomenon, but it is an improvement.

Optional Use

Use of uniform titles varies according to the size of the library. In Rule 25.1, "Use of Uniform Titles," use is defined as optional and each cataloging agency is advised to set its own policies. However, the requirement of the uniform title as the main entry in such cases as anonymous works, laws, etc. overrides the optional status of the uniform title as stated in Rule 25.1. Each library must examine the rules and decide which they will apply.

As in all the previous chapters, there are small changes, or expansions. Rule 25.3B, for instance, gives instructions on the selection of a uniform title when one has not been established.

Every library will use some of the uniform titles, particularly those which have become known through long use. Rule 25.2D broadens the provisions for added entries for the title proper. Added entries for the title are required whenever the uniform title is the main entry and even when it is a filing device. AACR 1 "preferred" an added entry for the title.

Major Changes

Several important changes have taken place in the rules for uniform titles. Parts of works with distinctive titles of their own and published separately must now be entered under their own title (Rule 25.6A1); it was an option in AACR 1 Rule 106. For example:

Old Form	**AACR 2 Form**
₍Canterbury tales. The knight's tale₎	₍The knight's tale₎
₍The lord of the rings. 2. The two towers₎	₍The two towers₎

However, separately published parts identified by a generalized term, such as "Part," or "Book," continue to be part of the uniform title for the whole work (Rule 25.6A2).

The new rules also make a clear distinction for publications which purport to be the complete works of an individual and a collection of selections (Rules 25.8 and 25.9). These rules also affect music titles. Here "Works" may now apply only to the complete works of a composer, according to Rule 25.8. "Selections" of either types of compositions or music for a given medium are governed by Rule 25.9, the general rule. Therefore a collection of compositions for a specific medium cannot have the uniform title "Works, . . ." Rule 25.36 requires that the uniform title be formulated giving only the medium.

Old Form	**AACR 2 Form**
₍Works, vocal₎	₍Vocal music₎
₍Works, piano₎	₍Piano music₎

This treatment of a collection of music for a medium of performance has been aligned to conform with the rules for collections of types of compositions (compare AACR 1 Rule 239D and AACR 2 Rule 25.36).

The rules for uniform titles for sacred scriptures have also been standardized. The separately published parts of non-Christian scriptures are now also entered under the title of the work of which they are a part (compare AACR 2 Rule 25.18F and AACR 1 Rule 116). An example of this change is given in Chapter VI, Example M9.

The other important changes were discussed in previous chapters. The form subheadings such as "Laws, Statutes, etc.," or "Liturgy and ritual" have been abandoned and uniform titles have taken their place. Most of these works will now receive a specific uniform title either as the main entry, as for Jewish liturgical works, or uniform titles for the specific liturgy or law.

The preferred form of a music uniform title is the composer's original title (see Example MU3). The text for selection of the uniform title in AACR 2 is less complex and may be a more efficient means of deciding on its form.

There are, of course, other changes, particularly in music uniform titles. A detailed analysis of these should be made by the music experts in the field.

IX

Catalogers' Aids

For librarians charged with the responsibility of providing access to a library's materials, AACR 2 will be the most important tool, but it alone will not suffice. It is not designed to answer and resolve *all* cataloging problems; other sources must be consulted.

In this section a selected number of works to aid in processing a title are given; these should be part of nearly any catalog department's handy reference collection. In addition, we should not overlook the various biographic sources, as well as general and subject encyclopedias and handbooks available on most reference shelves. A resourceful librarian should be able to find an answer to nearly every question that comes up in the process of cataloging by using the catalog he or she is helping to produce, and to work with the total collection to resolve most problems of identification. In some cases, of course, pertinent sources are not available, and making an independent decision to resolve a cataloging problem may be the most practical solution.

The majority of cataloging problems, however, can be resolved with rather everyday reference tools such as a general dictionary. *Webster's International Dictionary*—which AACR 2 accepts as the spelling authority—is essential, since it not only answers English orthographic riddles but even provides solutions to subject heading problems (e.g., scientific vs. vernacular names for insects, fish, plants, etc.). Also available should be foreign language dictionaries, although their limitations must be recognized. It may be advisable to have more than one dictionary at hand for a particular language, particularly if the acquisitions in this language are heavy.

Below are listed, with annotations, some recommended sources for resolving cataloging questions. (Sources are given in AACR 2 rather than standard bibliographic format.)

STYLE AND NONPRESCRIBED PUNCTUATION

A manual of style : for authors, editors and copywriters. -- 12 ed. rev. and enl. -- Chicago : University of Chicago Press, 1969. -- ix, 546 p.

[Commonly called the *Chicago Style Manual*. The 13th edition
is to be published in 1981.]

This style manual was one of the titles used to reconcile the British and North American texts of AACR 1, and it should also be consulted (see Rule 0.11 of AACR 2) when the rules do not treat a particular aspect of style or punctuation.

The second part of the current Chicago *Manual,* on "Style," is especially useful to the cataloging librarian. The following aspects are particularly noteworthy:

Punctuation. The treatment of punctuation is concise, easily understood and applied.

Names and Terms. The *Manual* contains a very useful compilation of capitalization problems of all types of names, including place names, which is helpful when transcribing titles and other title information, particularly for foreign languages. Included are foreign language derivatives. (Note that AACR 2's Appendix A is the *primary* source for capitalization in catalog records for English and foreign languages.)

Foreign Languages in Type. The idiosyncracies of the most frequently encountered languages are discussed here. The information given is useful for transcribing data from the title page; even word division is included. Transliteration tables for Russian and Greek are also given. Librarians should, however, use the ALA/LC tables for all transliterations. (Further discussion on transliteration appears later in this chapter.)

Mathematics in Type. This section is very important for the description of mathematical symbols not reproducible in type; several tables with symbols and their meaning are given.

Style manual. -- Rev. ed. -- Washington : For sale by the
Supt. of Docs., G.P.O., 1973. -- viii, 548 p.

[Generally known as the *G.P.O. Style Manual.*]

The *G.P.O. Style Manual* was the guide for style and punctuation for AACR 1, North American edition. Although no longer the AACR 2 official source, it has not lost its usefulness. All aspects of the mechanics of writing are considered in this volume which treats common difficulties with the English language in greater detail than does the 12th edition of the *Chicago Style Manual.* The section on signs and symbols is a great deal broader, including mathematical symbols as well as signs of measure, money, planets, sex, shapes, soils, etc.

LIBRARY AND BOOK WORLD TERMINOLOGY

Harrod, Leonard Montague. The librarian's glossary of
terms used in librarianship, documentation and the book
crafts and reference books. -- Boulder, CO. : Westview
Press, 1977. -- 903 p.

This glossary is useful for any librarian, but particularly for the novice librarian becoming familiar with the jargon of the profession and learning about the physical book. Terminology used in all areas of librarianship is succinctly explained. The new areas of automation, indexing and nonprint media are also included. Most pertinent to the cataloging process, however, is the information relating to the book itself.

The *ALA Glossary of Library Terms* by Elizabeth H. Thompson (168 p.) still has some useful information but the 1943 imprint date certainly does not make it the most current or authoritative work on library terminology. A revised edition is expected to be published at the end of 1981.

FOREIGN LANGUAGE BOOK AND PUBLISHING TERMINOLOGY

> Dictionarium bibliothecarii practicum : ad usum
> internationalem in XXII linguis = The librarian's
> practical dictionary : in 22 languages = Wörterbuch
> des Bibliothekars : in 22 Sprachen / edited by
> Zoltan Pipico. -- 6th rev. & enl. ed. -- Pullach,
> München : Verlag Dokumentation, 1974. -- 385 p.

This dictionary lists English-language terms of the book, library and publishing worlds. Each English term is followed by its equivalent in 21 languages. The most commonly encountered languages (including Russian) are presented first. To provide access to the languages, each term has been arranged in its own alphabetical sequence with a reference number for the English word. The work is quite restrictive, since only one meaning or equivalent is given when more may be required. There are no explanations for usage.

> Dictionary of library science, information and documentation
> in six languages : English/American - French - Spanish -
> Italian - Dutch and German / compiled and arranged on an
> English alphabetical basis by W.F. Clason ; with Arabic
> supplement by Shawky Salem. -- Amsterdam ; New York :
> Elsevier Scientific Publ. Co., 1976. -- 908 p.

This dictionary is precisely what its title says. Its usefulness to a cataloging librarian lies in the fact that it deals with the most frequently-encountered foreign terms and languages from the library's point of view. Cataloging in a language in which only a basic knowledge has been acquired makes the book a helpful tool, since the average dictionary seldom covers enough book-related terms. However, only one term per language is given, without explanation for usage, so that a general dictionary is recommended for a more complete definition.

FOREIGN LANGUAGE MANUALS

> Allen, C.G. A manual of European languages for libraries. --
> 3rd impression with minor correct. -- London ; New York :
> Bowker in association with the London School of Economics,
> 1978, c1975. -- xiii, 803 p.

This manual is arranged by language groups and treats a language's general characteristics, "bibliolinguistics" (patterns found in bibliographic data), orthography and word division. The inclusion of grammar, phonetics and a glossary of bibliographic terms is most helpful. Since the book is limited to European languages it can give more detail about a particular language. This title can be very useful to those who have studied at least one foreign language.

> von Ostermann, Georg F. Manual of foreign languages,
> for the use of librarians, bibliographers, research
> workers, editors, translators and printers. -- 4th
> ed., rev. and enl. -- New York : Central Book Co.,
> 1952. -- 414 p.

The von Ostermann title has been the standard foreign language manual for several generations of librarians and still has not lost its usefulness. It contains 141 languages, including African and American Indian languages. Even "Wendish" has not been neglected (although hardly a handful of these people still exist)! Grammatical idiosyncracies, orthography, capitalization, pronunciation and diacritical marks are discussed for each language. Romanization is also given; however, the ALA/LC transliteration tables are the authority in this area and von Ostermann's romanization should not be applied (see below).

TRANSLITERATION

> Cataloging service / Processing Department, Library
> of Congress. -- Bulletin no. 118 (summer 1976)-no. 125
> (spring 1978). -- Washington : Cataloging Distribution
> Service, Library of Congress, 1976-1978.

> Cataloging service bulletin / Processing Services,
> Library of Congress. -- no. 1 (summer 1978)-
> Washington : The Library, 1978-

The ALA/LC transliteration tables are the sources for romanization for languages in non-Roman alphabets; they are also given as the sources in AACR 2 (see Rule 0.13, Language Preferences). The first tables were published in LC's *Bulletin*, no. 118; the most recent one was issued in the *Cataloging Service Bulletin*, no. 5 and is for Ottoman Turkish.

The *Bulletin* changed title with no. 125 and is now called *Cataloging Service Bulletin*; hence the two citations. Like its predecessor, it may be obtained directly from the Library of Congress and is, at present, free of charge. (See Chapter X for additional information.)

UNREPRODUCIBLE SYMBOLS

Placing square brackets around the descriptions of symbols which cannot be reproduced with available typographic facilities is a longstanding cataloging practice and remains part of the rules. Many of these symbols are scientific or mathematical and may vary slightly in meaning from discipline to discipline. Since few librarians have an extensive scientific background, the appropriate sources must be consulted to do the job as correctly as possible. There are some standard general sources, some general scientific sources and the standard handbooks for a given discipline in which the description for these symbols may be located. A few samples follow.

General Sources

> Dreyfuss, Henry. Symbol source book : an authoritative
>   guide to international graphic symbols / Henry Dreyfuss.
>   -- New York : McGraw-Hill, 1972. -- 292 p.

> Shepherd, Walter. Shepherd's glossary of graphic signs and
>   symbols / compiled and classified for ready reference by
>   Walter Shepherd. -- London : J.M. Dent, 1971. --
>   x, 597 p.

General Science

> McGraw-Hill dictionary of scientific and technical terms /
>   David M. Lapedes, editor in chief. -- 2nd ed. -- New York
>   : McGraw-Hill, c1978. -- xv, 1771, A58 p.

> Van Nostrand's scientific encyclopedia / edited by Douglas
>   M. Considine. -- 5th ed. -- New York : Van Nostrand Reinhold,
>   1976. -- xi, 2370 p.

Special Topical

> CRC handbook of tables for mathematics / Robert C. Weast,
>   editor-in-chief ; Samuel M. Salby, editor-in-chief for
>   mathematics. -- Rev. 4th ed. -- Cleveland, Ohio : CRC Press,
>   1975. -- 1125 p.

> CRC handbook of chemistry and physics : a ready reference
>   book of chemical and physical data / editor Robert C. Weast ;
>   associate editor Melvin J. Astle. -- 60th ed., 1979-1980.
>   -- Boca Raton, FL. : CRC Press, 1979. -- 2447 p. in
>   various pagings.

Geographic Names

The U.S. Board of Geographic names' *Gazetteers* have been the authoritative sources for geographic names in the United States for some time and are listed as such in AACR 1. AACR 2, being an international code, does not mention the Board, but recommends the use of gazetteers or other reference sources and advocates the English form over the vernacular in nearly all cases.

The Library of Congress will continue use of the Board's *Gazetteers* but with some modification (see *Cataloging Service Bulletin,* no. 6, fall 1979). The Board's *Gazetteers* continue to be excellent sources for all types of geographic names not easily located elsewhere. Each *Gazetteer* is dedicated to a specific country or group of countries, region or topographic feature. LC staff uses the *Rand McNally Commercial Atlas and Marketing Guide* as the authoritative source for names of counties, a practice which can easily be adapted since most libraries that do original cataloging probably own this title.

The *Columbia Lippincott Gazetteer of the World* is an old standby and still good for answering many questions. However, it must be used with great caution since many of the African countries and other areas of the world have undergone political and name changes.

The latest encyclopedias, atlases or maps will, of course, provide the most current information.

CATALOGING RULES: AACR 1 VS. AACR 2

Where's that rule? : a cross-index of the two editions
of the Anglo-American cataloguing rules / by Ronald
Hagler. -- Ottawa : Canadian Library Association,
1979. -- 127 p. ; 25 cm. -- "Incorporating a commen-
tary on the second edition and on changes from previous cataloging standards."

Hagler's *Where's That Rule?* is very useful for applying the new code. In this small volume Hagler has compiled a very practical cross-index to both editions of AACR, enabling us to find a corresponding rule in either edition.

Let's take the uniform title as an example. We may wish to know AACR 2's counterpart for Rule 233A, choice of language for the uniform title; by looking up 233A, we will find that the equivalent in AACR 2 is Rule 25.27A. Conversely, we will be able to learn that the equivalent of 25.27A is 233A and that we are also dealing with a change in the choice of language for the uniform title.

This volume is more than a cross-index. Hagler also explains and discusses many changes from an insider's vantage point, since he was a member of the Joint Steering Committee for the code revision.

ILLUSTRATING THE RULES

A number of titles illustrating the new rules have already appeared on the market; we will name only two of them.

Maxwell, Margaret F. Handbook for AACR2 : explaining and
illustrating Anglo-American cataloging rules : second
edition / by Margaret F. Maxwell. -- Chicago : American
Library Association, 1980. -- xi, 463 p. ; 25 cm.

The most recent publication is Maxwell's *Handbook for AACR 2.* It is large in scope and detail, and the historical perspectives add an additional dimension. All formats presented in AACR 2 are represented in this volume; the six chapters of AACR 2 which cover the access points and their form are each treated in separate chapters. There are many examples illustrating the various rules and different aspects of cataloging. Clearly, a great deal of scholarly effort lies behind the text of this handbook.

Hunter, Eric J. Examples illustrating AACR2 / Eric J.
Hunter and Nicholas J. Fox. -- Chicago : American Library
Association distributor ; London : Library Association,
1980. -- 192 p. ; 24 cm.

Another useful title is the Hunter/Fox *Examples Illustrating AACR2.* It contains cataloging examples which illustrate a variety of cataloging problems and is arranged by main entry in alphabetical order.

THEORETICAL BASIS FOR AACR 2

In the summer of 1980, the American Library Association published *The Making of a Code: The Issues Underlying AACR 2,* a collection of papers presented at the International Conference on AACR 2 in Tallahassee, FL in March 1979. Edited by Doris Hargrett Clack, the book contains papers by 14 noted cataloging authorities. Those interested in understanding the theory behind the rules and the reasoning that led to various rule revisions will find this an excellent source of information.

CONCISE AACR 2

Gorman's *Concise AACR 2* is to be published toward the end of 1980 by the American Library Association. This title will probably be most useful to those individuals who must occasionally catalog an item for a small library and for whom the full text of the code may be unnecessarily cumbersome. The text will include examples to illustrate the rules.

SPECIAL CATALOGING MANUALS

Two special cataloging manuals are in progress, one for cartographic material and the other for government publications. Both will be published by the American Library Association. The manual for cartographic material should be released toward the end of 1980, and the government publications one early in 1981. The ALA literature should announce their publication and cost.

Library of Congress published *Special Problems in Serial Cataloging,* 1979, which is a most useful aid, but regrettably only deals with problems related to AACR 1. In its preface LC indicated that it *may* issue other tools of this nature; therefore, it is advisable to monitor the *Library of Congress Information Bulletin* for the new LC publications column.

X

Afterword: Keeping Up with the Changes

Libraries and cataloging practices have changed continually through the years. As libraries evolved from repositories for the safekeeping of books for the privileged few to public places with access to all, the cataloging process underwent equally dramatic changes. First were simple book lists in which bookmen advertised their wares. Those catalogs grew from handwritten alphabetical lists to card catalogs, initially produced in a fancy "library hand," until LC's printed cards and typewritten cards appeared. Today catalog cards are prepared with high-speed printers, which fuse print to a surface; and whole catalogs are produced in microform or as online bibliographic data bases.

Descriptive cataloging, as we know it, began with Panizzi's "91 Theses" in 1841. Since then, these basic rules have grown in complexity and have undergone numerous revisions. Thus it is not likely that we have now arrived at the final stage of rules for description and access to materials gathered in libraries. An important aspect of bibliographic description—the machine-readable record and computer retrieval capabilities—has not been fully addressed by AACR 2. Moreover, much bibliographic data is no longer prepared by and for one location, but has become machine interchangeable between nations and languages. These changes are beginning to be reflected in cataloging practices, and AACR 2 is only the start of a second evolutionary change in bibliographic access and exchange. Revisions dealing with these new forms of data preparation and dissemination should be expected.

One criticism of AACR 2 has been that the new rules are not anticipating future data processing changes in libraries, and that perhaps they have not even caught up with the present. Although very few libraries have begun using the code, proposals for changes are already being developed. The National Library of Canada and the Library of Congress are working with *Guidelines for the Formulation of Unique Titles,* published in *Cataloging Service Bulletin,* no. 5, summer 1979. The guidelines deal with the problem of distinguishing one like title from another for series and serials; this is of particular importance for online bibliographic data, its display and retrieval.

The microform publishing community disagrees very much with the manner in which microforms are being cataloged. AACR 2 requires that all information about the original publication appear in the note area; the concern is that this important bibliographic information about the original is not readily available to the user. The pressure from this group has been strong and persistent enough to have the American Library Association's Cataloging Committee on Description and Access (RTSD, CCS*) study the problem for a possible recommendation at ALA's annual meeting in June-July 1980. This could result in a change, some time in the future, in the rules on description of microforms.

Not all of us will have equal access to this information, but it is important in order to process materials accurately, particularly when bibliographic records must be added to a nationwide data base. Here the individual's responsibility to the whole, the cooperative spirit of the professional, is challenged. But librarians can stay informed. The Library of Congress in the past published changes to AACR 1 in its *Cataloging Service Bulletin,* and will continue to do so for AACR 2. The winter 1980 issue, for example, carried news of an additional change (or interpretation, as it is called) to AACR 2. This change expands the rule on entry under corporate body so that cartographic materials would also be included and receive entry under a corporate name. Other pertinent rule interpretations regarding entry of maps under corporate names and unique titles for serials and series will be published before 1981.

At irregular intervals the Library of Congress publishes proposals for change, rule interpretations (as was the case for AACR 1, Chapter 6, rev.), and other important cataloging news in its weekly *Library of Congress Information Bulletin* (LCIB). A weekly publication, the *Information Bulletin* may disseminate information more quickly than the quarterly *Cataloging Service Bulletin.*

Both of these publications should be available to the cataloging librarian. As of now they are free and easily obtainable. For your convenience the titles and addresses are listed below:

> *Cataloging Service Bulletin*
> Available from:
> > Cataloging Distribution Service
> > Library of Congress
> > Building 159, Navy Yard Annex
> > Washington, DC 20541
>
> *Library of Congress Information Bulletin*
> Available from:
> > Information Office
> > Library of Congress
> > Washington, DC 20540

LC's rule interpretations are as important as changes to the rules themselves and will no doubt play a vital role in the application of AACR 2 in U.S. libraries of all types and sizes. Although LC is certainly not the only employer of competent catalog librarians, it processes more and a greater variety of materials than any other organization. It thus has at its disposal a large, cumulative number of years of experience to make judicious decisions and

---

*Resources and Technical Services Division, Cataloging and Classification Section.

to give sound interpretations of the rules. Perhaps even more significant is that the three online utilities (WLN, RLIN and OCLC), which make catalog data available to the library community, load the MARC tapes onto their data bases. Librarians who use this data for catalog production, and who want to build a new consistent catalog according to the new rules, will find it essential to incorporate LC's interpretations into their local cataloging practices.

Those interested in the activities of more distant cataloging librarians and the changes, problems and solutions they have reached may wish to consult *International Cataloguing*, published by the Universal Bibliographic Control office in London, particularly since the activities of the IFLA Committee on Cataloguing are reported there. The committee's activities have strongly influenced the new code and are likely to precipitate new ideas and resolutions to problems from an international point of view.

Notes

Chapter I

1. Michael Gorman and Paul W. Winkler, eds., *Anglo-American Cataloguing Rules,* 2nd ed. (Chicago: American Library Association, Ottawa: Canadian Library Association, London: The Library Association, 1978).

2. *Cataloging Service Bulletin,* no. 7 (winter 1980).

3. *Anglo-American Cataloging Rules.* North American Text. Chapter 6, revised (Chicago: American Library Association, 1974).

Chapter III

1. *Cataloging Service Bulletin,* no. 2 (fall 1978): 18-23.

2. C.A. Cutter, *Rules for a Dictionary Catalog,* 4th ed. (Washington, DC: Government Printing Office), pp. 18-23.

3. M. Gorman, "The Anglo-American Cataloguing Rules, Second Edition," *Library Resources & Technical Services,* Vol. 22, No. 3 (summer 1979): 215.

4. *Cataloging Service Bulletin,* no. 7 (winter 1980), contains an announcement by the Library of Congress that *National Level Bibliographic Record—Books,* a looseleaf service, is under development.

Chapter IV

1. Working Group on the General International Standard Bibliographic Description, *ISBD (G): General International Standard Bibliographic Description: Annotated Text* (London: IFLA International Office for UBC, 1977), p. 5.

2. *ISBD (M): International Standard Bibliographic Description for Monographic Description,* 1st standard ed., rev. (London: IFLA International Office for UBC, 1978), p. 11, and Joint Working Group on the International Standard Bibliographic Description for Serials, *ISBD (S): International Standard Bibliographic Description for Serials,* 1st standard ed. (London: IFLA International Office for UBC, 1977), pp. 10-11.

Chapter V

1. *ISBD (M),* p. 1.

Chapter VI

1. *Cataloging Service Bulletin,* no. 8 (spring 1980): 13.

2. Ibid.

Chapter VII

1. International Conference on Cataloguing Principles, Paris, October 9-18, 1961, *Report* (London: International Federation of Library Associations, 1963), pp. 68-74.

2. See footnote 25, *Anglo-American Cataloging Rules.* North American Text (Chicago: American Library Association, 1967), p. 66.

Chapter VIII

1. W.G. Potter, "When Names Collide: Conflicts in the Catalog and AACR 2," *Library Resources & Technical Services,* Vol. 24, No. 1 (winter 1980): 3-16.

2. Arlene Taylor Dowell, at the 1980 Annual ALA Conference, New York, presented statistics which corroborate this assumption, except for small libraries, which anticipate an increase in changes towards the end of the first five years after implementation of AACR 2.

3. J.A. Hewitt and D.E. Gleim, "The Case for Not Closing the Catalog," *American Libraries,* Vol. 10, No. 3 (March 1979): 120.

4. The "Old Form" and the "AACR 2 Form" headings for this and the following listings have been taken from *Cataloging Service Bulletin,* no. 6 (fall 1979): 226-40 and no. 8 (spring 1980): 15-24. The uniform law title examples are our own. LC has not yet included such headings in its published documentation.

5. Ibid.

6. *Cataloging Service Bulletin,* no. 6 (fall 1979): 10, instructs LC staff to include works published during and after a person's lifetime in his or her language.

7. Ibid. LC has very specific instructions for applying Rule 22.3A to living persons. The second choice, the latest form, is to be ignored and the fullest form should be used. Otherwise, when no clear decision can be made—i.e., when two thirds of the sources do not have the same form—the fullest form, the third choice, is used to establish a name.

8. AACR 1 (1967), Alternative Rule 42B.

9. *Cataloging Service Bulletin,* no. 8 (spring 1980): 13.

10. *Cataloging Service Bulletin,* no. 6 (fall 1979): 15.

Acknowledgements

Fortuna and Opportuna made possible the commencement and conclusion of this work. Arlene Dowell is to be thanked for being Fortuna, and it is hoped that her trust has been merited. Ellen Lazer, Opportuna and editor, must be thanked for her endurance with a novice author and attention to the development of the manuscript. Adrienne Hickey, copy and production editor, who had to contend with English as a second language as well as cataloging's prescribed and unprescribed punctuation, is also due a note of appreciation. To Inge Worth, a friend, my thanks for the "first aid" with the initial manuscript.

Thanks to Dr. Ann Painter, my teacher, who taught cataloging with a common sense approach and made her students aware of the divergent practices in existence throughout the library world; she permitted a questioning student to broaden her outlook and see beyond the confines of the 3 x 5 cataloger's world.

Real moral support throughout the process of writing and putting this little oeuvre together was given by Lois McCune; it was often more than needed and is greatly appreciated. Another supporter, particularly during the work on the later parts of the book, was Kay R. Lundy; my thanks to her as well. Diane Kloepper's efforts in typing the manuscript are also highly valued.

*   *   *   *

The author and editors of this book gratefully acknowledge the contribution of Richard J. Hyman, Director, Graduate School of Library and Information Studies, Queens College of the City University of New York. His comprehensive, responsive review and attention to both technical and editorial details of the manuscript are much appreciated.

General Index

Index to Rules

About the Author

Christa F. B. Hoffmann is LIRS (Library Information Retrieval System) Bibliographic Data Base Development and Quality Control Coordinator at the University of Nebraska, Lincoln Libraries, where for five years she was head of the Processing Division. Professional activities include appointments to OCLC's Internetwork Quality Control Council and the ALA RTSD/CCS Committee on Cataloging: Description and Access.

Ms. Hoffman worked as science cataloger, humanities librarian and reference librarian after earning her M.A. in Library Science in 1968 from Indiana University. She received a B.A. in history, government and English in 1965 from Wilmington College. Born in Germany, she emigrated to the U.S. in 1959 and became a citizen in 1965.